Thi

Terry Jordan grew up in the Fifties not far from the setting of Marianne's story.

She lives in North London, and after many changes in career direction she now mostly writes for a living. Her main interest is divining the future, at which she is *sometimes* quite successful.

*Growing up in the Fifties* is her second Optima book. Her first, *Agony Columns 1890-1980*, was published in 1988.

# GROWING UP
# IN THE
# FIFTIES

TERRY JORDAN

An OPTIMA Book

© Terry Jordan 1990

First published in 1990 by
Macdonald Optima, a division of
Macdonald & Co. (Publishers) Ltd

A member of Maxwell Macmillan Pergamon Publishing Corporation

British Library Cataloguing in Publication Data

Jordan, Terry
    Growing up in the fifties.
    1. Great Britain. Social life, 1950-1959
    I. Title
    941.0855

    ISBN 0-356-15553-6


Macdonald & Co. (Publishers) Ltd
Orbit House
1 New Fetter Lane
London EC4A 1AR

Typeset in Century Schoolbook by
Leaper & Gard Ltd, Bristol

Made and printed in Great Britain by
The Guernsey Press Co. Ltd., Guernsey, Channel Islands.

*The Publishers would like to thank Penguin Books Ltd
for permission to reproduce the Penguin Book cover.
Cover photographs from Macdonald Aldus Archive.*

# CONTENTS

# INTRODUCTION

The first reaction of many people when asked to recall the Fifties is, 'Nothing happened. Well, it was after the War and before the Sixties. It was dull.' They see those years as one long yawn, as nondescript as a new town and as boring as the bombsites that still depressed the landscape. In retrospect, the decade of the Fifties proves more than just the transition between War and 'Give Peace a Chance'. It introduced teenagers, commercial jet travel and the M1. And what about television? It seems laughable now that early TV was considered a novelty. The small screen in a big box replaced the fireplace and radio as the focus for family life and by mid-decade almost half of British households owned a set. You could walk down any residential street at dusk and the eerie glow from the many small screens showed the new way leisure time was being spent. As a consequence, cinema audiences stayed at home and Michael Balcon was forced to sell his Ealing Studios (home of the successful Ealing comedies) to the BBC.

A key to understanding life in the Fifties may be the concept of Lifestyle. People wanted and expected to improve their living standards, expected that their children would be educated. The big leap in status from working to middle class was within grasp – not for the parents, of course, but for their children, born into a National Health system, who would take the eleven-plus exam and then, from 1951, their GCEs. With such a sound and equitable start to life, anything, *within reason*, was possible. Girls were expected to support themselves between school and marriage, but not encouraged to aspire towards a profession. Careers counselling was as non-existent as sex education, and this generation of girls was to be kept innocent of both the physical and the financial facts of life.

There is usually one event which really initiates a

decade and for the people of Britain it has to be the death of George VI in February 1952. The coronation of his pretty, newly wed daughter, Queen Elizabeth, was cheered by the many loyal subjects who jammed along the procession route. But many more crowded into a neighbour's home to watch the pageantry on television and had a better, if monochromic, view. After fifty years of kings, the symbolism of a young glamorous Queen couldn't have been lost on the nation's girls. Elizabeth II showed the world that a woman was up to the task of leading a major country, even if it wasn't Victoria's vast Empire.

Winston Churchill was for the last time prime minister from 1951, sandwiching the Attlee post-war Labour government. In America, Dwight Eisenhower held the highest office from 1952 and Richard Nixon was his vice-president. Throughout the Fifties, in Britain, there were to be successive Conservative governments. After Churchill, we remember Eden for the infamous hash of the Suez Crisis (1956). With the French and Israelis, Britain's unsuccessful move to occupy the Suez Canal Zone attracted censure by the United Nations and world-wide disapproval. Then there was Macmillan, elected the following year.

Most believed Harold Macmillan when he told the country in 1957 that they had 'never had it so good': 38 per cent owned their own homes, wages had risen since 1950 by 34 per cent and the future seemed as wholesome as the Enid Blyton stories parents read to their children at bedtime. But others found life at home lacking in opportunity and they sought sun and space abroad in Australia or New Zealand, often on ten-pound assisted-passage schemes. For the same reasons, many black Commonwealth immigrants arrived in Britain to take up the hundreds of (usually low-paid) jobs that were on offer. Once they had saved enough to send for their families, the first numbers of black children took their chances growing up in Britain. It didn't always go easily – acceptance sometimes wasn't forthcoming and fear and suspicion led to racial rioting in Nottingham and Notting Hill in 1958.

During the Fifties, most of Africa and the Far East gained independence and Empire Day was more accurately retitled Commonwealth Day.

If anything is the real landmark of the Fifties, it is the emergence of the teenager, both as a cult and a market force. The Teddy Boy style with its drape jackets and crêpe-soled shoes was well entrenched by 1955 and it only took Elvis Presley's 1956 recording of 'Heartbreak Hotel' to touch off the rock 'n' roll craze. Girl teens were creating their own styles, including enormous skirts flounced out by petticoats and hair backcombed up to a rock-hard bubble. Also in 1956, James Dean appeared in the film *Rebel Without a Cause*, and John Osborne's play *Look Back in Anger* launched a generation of writers whose alienation from mainstream society resulted in their collective name, 'Angry Young Men'.

1955/56 seems pivotal, both for progress and uncertainty, as the first nuclear power station came into controversial operation at Calder Hall. People had taken the post-war world much in their stride though many were uneasy about the Cold War. A Europe split by the Iron Curtain raised serious doubts about a lasting peace. The Campaign for Nuclear Disarmament, with the Aldermaston marches and Trafalgar Square rallies in the late Fifties, supplied an alternative political view, one that said the devastation of Hiroshima and Nagasaki must never happen again. And over thirty years later, the debate is still going on.

If you are old enough to think back on the Fifties, you'll remember much that was dreary, hopefully more that was fun. Most of us have mixed feelings about the time of our childhoods. The seven girls whose stories make this book may add to your memories of how we lived, by understanding what it was like for someone else. The years are long gone but Fifties' style remains in view, suspended in film and in vinyl and recycled periodically through the media. It's easy to believe the myths. This book tells it how it really was (at least for seven girls) to be growing up in the Fifties.

# HAZEL

What brings the Fifties to mind really well for me is the petticoats. I used to wear lots of them and that's what Fifties' fashion was all about. We went jiving a lot and it was our favourite recreation. I had started jiving in 1952 at fourteen-and-a-half and, to me, the fun part of the Fifties was those petticoats. You could style yourself a Teddy Girl, or you wore lots of petticoats and lots of frills, and there was nothing to stop you actually doing both! The Teddy Girl outfit was real smart, and the threat of flick knives and all the sorts of things that went with it, was terribly exciting. I went round with a group of Teds in Torquay when I was sixteen. My family moved from Manchester to Devon where I got mixed up with this gang. It would have horrified my parents had they known. Prejudice? People expected you to go around ripping up cinema seats. Our lot never did it but we had motorbikes and dressed the part. I never thought Teddy Boys were all they were cracked up to be. Not in my area anyway. They were pussy cats, and although some of them carried weapons, the knives were just for show. The most traumatic event that happened to us was when a friend of my boyfriend's got killed on his motorbike. That really sobered us all up, settled us down a bit for a time. We realized we were living very high.

The boys varied so much. I don't think I had an 'ideal man', though. I just sort of fell in and out of love willy-nilly in my early teens and it was an ongoing thing. Some were from school and they could be chess players and we would spend a nice evening at one or another's house playing chess. I'd get teased and the other lads in the school used to say, 'You were playing Chest, we know!' But it was all innocent, a kiss and a hug at the end of the evening. As I grew a bit older, I found that from being an ugly duckling, I became quite pretty. I suffered from puppy fat when we moved down to Devon, and almost overnight I changed. It wasn't until somebody took a photograph of me that I thought, 'Gosh, that's not half bad!' By that time, I had had my hair cut and had miraculously lost weight. I was used to teasing and all of a sudden it stopped as I became an Extremely Desirable Object! It was magic!

My hair was very short, straight with a parting, but generally it was much the same shape as it is now. To my godson's christening, when I was seventeen, I wore a pale lilac dress, A-line, with a dropped waistline, lots of skirt, lots of frills underneath, and a hat that I made myself with strips of satin and ribbon and a bunch of lilac on the side. Everybody said I looked more like a bride than a godmother, but this dress was absolutely typically Fifties. It had a cross-over bodice and was low cut. We tried to get away with showing as much bust as we could without being indecent. My mother would have disapproved, I am sure, had she seen that particular outfit, but then my mother disapproved of many things I did!

My family was Victorian middle class at its most hide-bound and never grew out of it. I pushed the boundaries out. My poor sister used to get thrashed for a lot of things and I saw that happen. In fact my mother was so sickened with it she never laid a finger on me. We used to argue instead and I was rebellious. The poor woman, I gave her a dreadful time. The teenage freedoms were just beginning. All my friends were getting record-players and having boyfriends in the home, making a noise. But I wasn't allowed to make a sound. If I ran through the sitting room, the floor used to spring, and Mother would say, 'Don't do that, the pictures will fall off the wall!' I just was not allowed free expression, either emotional or physical. The joys of spring were maintained outside the home but never within it. Everything was circumspect. This is not to say that it was loveless or that it wasn't fun at times, but it was very restrained.

Radio Luxembourg was the saving of me. I used to be told off at half past ten at night when I'd be studying by Radio Luxembourg. 'How can you possibly study your books with that racket going on? Turn it off!' It was all

Frankie Laine and 'I Believe'. Funnily, I didn't like Rock. I didn't even like Cliff Richard, who was not so clean cut in those days. I thought he was over the top at the time. I went in for Frankie Laine and Johnnie Brandon – I even have an autograph of Johnnie Brandon. I loved the big bands as well, like Dankworth, and I saw Satchmo, once.

As far as wearing make-up was concerned, Yardley had a club for teenage girls to teach us how to apply it properly. Every month I was sent a free sample of one of their products and lots of advice. Cosmetic houses don't do that now. I belonged to that club from fourteen onwards, although I wasn't supposed to wear make-up that young. It was very formative, very educational for me to learn to use cosmetics discreetly and how to look after my skin. My friends and I used to show off to each other what new make-up we had acquired in an 'aren't-you-jealous?' way. There was a lot of rivalry. The Yardley's club used to advertise in magazines and you paid a very nominal sum to join. Everything from there on in was free, it wasn't just to encourage you to buy their products. Right now there is a resurgence of the natural look and a lot of girls don't bother with make-up unless they are going somewhere very special. That's how we were. We had pink lipstick and mascara but eye shadow was considered a bit obvious. When we first put eye shadow on we went over the top through inexperience. I wouldn't put on my lipstick, anyway, until I left the house! I didn't wear anything on my skin, such as foundation or powder, just a little Nivea or lacto calamine if my skin became greasy. And I had a little green ladies' razor for my legs. Everyone had one. You could get blue or pink as well as green, but there wasn't anything else.

The magazine *She* came out when I was thirteen or fourteen, and I loved it. It cost a shilling out of my allowance of ten bob a week but it was dynamic compared with the other women's magazines. *She* had a lot of pizzaz and catered for the younger woman, be she married or in her teens, who wanted to know about fashion, and it was glossy. The glossies were normally for older women who had more money. *She* was everybody's glossy magazine. You could get *Woman, Woman's Own, Woman's Weekly, Titbits, Women's Friend* and *The Lady*, but they were all very traditional and *She* was something totally different. Mother got *Woman* and *Woman's Own*, but I don't know whether she took them for leisure or to learn new things.

Winklepickers ruined my feet and now I have bunions. The first pair of shoes I bought for myself were red leather. I had a real thing about having a pair of red leather shoes, after-school shoes. These had little bows, and the edges of the shoe and the bows had little white dots round them. I had to clean these shoes with red cleaner and pick out the dots with Meltonian White, afterwards, with a paint brush. That is how fussy I was about these red shoes. But I did this, went to this trouble, because these white dots filled up with polish. So I dug the polish out and dipped them with white Meltonian. I did this at least once a week. I spent all Saturday, until the evening, hoping that somebody would ask me for a date for that night and getting all ready for it. But I often didn't get asked anywhere, so would go down to the coffee bar, which was perhaps open until nine. I'd come home, disappointed, at quarter to ten on the last bus.

When I was in my last year of school, I think – and this is speaking from the point of view of most of the girls in my class to hear us talk – we wanted to get married. That was the be-all and end-all. Most of it, I realize now, was that we wanted to experience sex; we really were curious about it. We also wanted to get shot of these tyrannical parents of ours. My prime motivation, certainly, was to be independent of my parents. As far as sex went, I was simply told never to do it! There was much kissing behind the bike sheds and a fisherman used to come up and throw fish on my doorstep because he was too shy to ask me out. It was easy to say 'No' in those days because it was expected you would. That was the beauty of it. I suppose to a certain extent our belief in our sexual ability was never actually challenged. The main thing we were frightened of was getting pregnant. We were absolutely torn at times.

My first 'awakening' was with the Head Boy. Getting him was a big challenge. I can remember him seeing me to the ferry for Kingswear. We were standing in the bus shelter for ages. He had to tell me to shut up because everybody was listening to my moans and sighs, you know. This was the first time that I was aware of the physical power of sex. I mean, this poor boy was totally aroused and I had never had that experience before. I got completely carried away! It was fortunate really we couldn't do too much about it because it probably would have been 'end of story' much earlier than it was in the end. I was sixteen and it didn't really last long with him as I lost interest. At the demise of our relationship, I instigated a riot in the Fifth Form. Because we were making a noise he came through and tried to sort it out. He got bombarded with ink pellets and everything else we could lay our hands on. He had to pick up the big table to get through the room without getting hit! I was rabble-rousing because I had become totally contemptuous of him. It was really strange. Having got my man, I didn't want him. I had won my prize and once he placed me on a pedestal, I didn't want to know. We realized we had this power over the male of the species and we realized, also, that to step over the boundaries was dangerous and 'Mother wouldn't like it'. Boys had a lot more respect for us girls in those days.

If I was going to be back home late in the evenings from school, I would tell my parents I was going to the pictures with a boyfriend. I was very up front about it. But oh, cucumber sandwiches with the crusts cut off, and tea, if a boy came around. It was a special occasion, and they would make an effort for the chap, whatever he was like. To give my parents their due, I brought some pretty awful dross home on occasions. The one I didn't bring home was the coloured boxer I picked up in a fairground booth. Of course there was total racial prejudice. I did tell Mother that I was, in fact, seeing two of the boxers. I was absolutely mad about boxing. I thought the boxers were so brave and they took on all challengers, you know. I met them by just standing at the ringside. I would be there, perhaps the whole evening, paying my money and watching the boxing. It was just a phase I went through. They were older men and they were brave and bold. I would hide my eyes when one of them got beaten up, apparently dreadfully, but normally it was pretty innocuous stuff – nobody bled, nobody really got hurt. The boxers would probably have been in their early twenties to my fifteen. The white one was a bit of a fly-by-night but I knew it and was careful with him. He took me home several times, but again, it was, sort of, a kiss on the doorstep because I was a Nice Girl. The coloured one was more serious. All this happened just before I moved to London and when I got there, he actually sent me flowers and notes. He was hoping that I could see him fight at Wembley. I couldn't go but I listened to it on the radio. He was beaten and I was absolutely devastated because he was a charming man and I knew it was virtually the end of his career. He had just gone too far to survive after that particular moment of glory.

I was brought up a Methodist, and when I got a bit older, and we moved to Devon, I voluntarily joined the Church of England. I wanted more pomp and ceremony, it appealed to my faith in the drama, typically Aries. I became very involved, joining the choir and the bell-ringers. We used to get paid a shilling a week for attending and played lots of tricks on the choir boys. It was a thoroughly good time. I ripped the skin off my hands in my first experience with bell-ringing and was told I was extremely brave not to have let go! I ended up going out with the captain of the bell-ringers, who was an absolute lothario, and remember thinking very unchristian thoughts about my girlfriend because she was going out with him as well. That was hilarious! We thought it was rather irreligious to kiss in the church, but we did it anyway. I sort of confessed my sins in bed at night afterwards, thinking God would strike me dead for kissing in church. I did believe in God and still do. When I was confirmed into the Church of England, I felt truly sanctified.

I also was re-born with Billy Graham. This was the first time he came over to England, and I was recruited by a boy in the class above me who was the local policeman's son. It got rather boring, as they chased you interminably thereafter to try and make new recruits and join in with this, that and the other. But I liked a lot of the church life and the youth club. I don't go to church now because I cry in church and I think I know why: I feel there is too much now to confess. It's strange, I'm very liberated, very independent, but I still feel quite tied to religion and basically unworthy. I do feel very spiritual and that there is a lot that we don't know about.

I don't remember that much about the War because life was so much easier in the Fifties. There was still sweet rationing which lasted for a long time and was probably very good for us. I can obviously recall the deprivations of the wartime diet though we were better off than most. We ate a lot of potatoes, a lot of dried milk and rice. The Fifties were more relaxed as obviously we were coming out of the shortages. We got the 'New Look' – longer skirts, because there was more material about. Politically, I can vaguely remember my mother and father's concern about the Suez Canal, but politics didn't touch me an awful lot. We were teenagers and didn't care anything about it.

The King's death was announced in school when I was eleven. The Head came into my domestic science class and told us. You didn't see the Headmaster normally except in Assembly or if you were naughty. The whole school was very hushed and very reverent. Personally, it didn't touch me much. There was a feeling of rejuvenation that we had a young queen. We all thought, isn't she pretty! Hasn't she got a nice looking husband! Most of us anticipated that it was going to be lovely from there on in, not realizing the significance, or otherwise, of a queen as opposed to a king, and the fact that Parliament actually ran the country. It was all Princes on White Chargers at my age and an occasion for pageantry. Any political significance and awareness only came when I got married. Even at eighteen, I wasn't politically oriented, being more concerned with earning a living, in those days, in Bedsit-land in Earls Court.

When I was young, I read absolutely everything I could get my hands on – Dickens and Scott, Jane Austen – and Enid Blyton as well! Lewis Carroll, all the classics, and I read (as everyone did) far in advance of what kids read now. I even read Thackeray. I suppose we read so much and read so well because there was no television. I wasn't allowed to listen to the radio much, either. Even though I went to a private school rather than a state school, there wasn't much in the way of mental stimulation. I also had a natural ability to read and could read before I went to school. One of my favourite games was 'Librarians'. My parents bought a job lot of books, old books, which they probably got for a few pennies. But in this lot were Scott and Thackeray and Dickens. I can remember reading these books and thinking that I must read them again when I got older because I didn't understand all of it. I had a love of the written word. Language is very important to me and I get very cross with TV announcers who don't adhere to English grammar.

When I got to *that* age, I used Tampax as soon as I could get rid of the conventional means my mother pressed upon me. I made my own decision on that very quickly, which was a problem because I kept on blocking the loo and didn't want to tell her why! We had old plumbing! I didn't feel embarrassed about going out and buying Tampax. It was a question of it being the lesser of the evils because sanitary towels were so obnoxious. I didn't fancy using Lil-lets, though. There was that slight difference and they were more for 'modern women', not teenagers. Most girls still used sanitary towels and I was quite out on a limb. Their mothers probably gave them dire warnings. I suspect they wanted them to be obviously virginal when they got married. My mother didn't state a case, pro or con, but didn't know that I would go and buy Tampax. Gradually, she must have realized, though, and if I asked her for money for supplies, she would just give it to me. It became accepted that I wouldn't have to pay for my own although, initially, I had to. I don't recall she ever asked if I was buying sanitary towels or Tampax. She wouldn't have discussed that sort of thing with me, it was too delicate. From that point of view, I was advantaged in that I was not monitored in such matters. I did get fed up with being told that Tampax didn't go down the loo and that they had to be burned down the garden in the incinerator. This meant that my father knew every time that I was in that situation, which I hated. As far as I was concerned, Tampax was the best thing since sliced bread, which only preceded it by a short while!

I was amazed when my parents let me move to London at seventeen. I hadn't gone on to university or college as the school wanted me to do basically because I thought my parents were mean and I would continue to go without all the things my working friends had. Mum and Dad weren't actually mean, just careful with money. A school leaver had several options. She could be a nurse or a secretary or a clerk, or she could go on to university or college. Absolutely nobody told me what I could expect at college. Nobody gave me any pointers at all. I didn't want to do anything that I thought a college qualification would prepare me to do. I didn't want to teach. What I didn't know about, and what people have career counselling for, nowadays, was the vast number of things I might have done with a degree, and I often regret not going on to further education. At that point, I wanted to either be a policewoman or an air hostess! I was too short to be a policewoman and they said, 'Go and do some typing and we might take you in the office. Then if you grow, you could be a policewoman in time.' In fact, I shrank. I thought this was very unkind of them. I'm glad I didn't do it. I couldn't be a policewoman now, although they were a bit more sheltered, then. To be an air hostess in the Fifties, you had to have two or three languages and have some kind of nursing qualification. It incensed me twenty years later when I discovered that one of my girlfriends, who hadn't got any of these (and was enormous), had been recruited by British Airways. And you had to be five foot, five. Again, I didn't qualify on height at five foot, three-and-a-half. I only had one language, French, and no nursing qualifications. It was very strict.

So the option when I left school was to take a clerical position. This satisfied my parents because it was decent and honourable. I went to work for the Gas Board in Torquay as a cost clerk. It was terribly boring stuff. You added thirty-three-and-a-third per cent profit to everything that was costed out on the estimates. I spent all day doing that. I lasted a year and then a girlfriend I had been at school with, who had moved to Uxbridge, said, 'Come and stay with me for a couple of weeks.' When I saw London, I didn't want to leave. I twisted my parents' arms and amazingly they let me leave home on the proviso I got a job first.

I waltzed into Derry and Tom's and got myself a job in the accounting department, just like that. My parents wanted me to live in the hostel immediately but oddly the hostel wouldn't take girls under eighteen. This seemed an irony, in a way, because it is when you're younger that you need the attention. Well, I got digs in Putney. I was earning the princely sum of two pounds, ten shillings a week and fares cost me ten bob a week from Putney to Earls Court. I paid twenty-five shillings a week for the room and put a shilling in the meter for hot water. And I froze and I starved. Fortunately, my mother pulled strings and got me an early place in the hostel in a few months because I wouldn't be here now if she hadn't! It was really dreadful. We used to have pie mash and peas in the ABC for a shilling, lunchtimes, or take our own sandwiches. In the evening, I would have something on toast or soup. My mother sent me enough food parcels over a period to keep me going and so did my sister, even though she couldn't afford it. Occasionally, I would splurge at the weekend and go and stay with my sister in Oxfordshire.

While I was in digs, it was very difficult to meet boys. I didn't feel brave enough to go out alone and I used to go straight home from work and be 'mis'. I don't even remember that I had a radio. I used to write long long letters home, which I still have. Six months later, when I moved into the hostel, everything changed because we girls used to go out in a group. The trouble I got into over two Persian boys I met in the post office! They seemed like nice lads and I had every confidence in my own ability to keep evil at bay, so to speak, but unfortunately, they got a bit naughty in the way that Persians will and said, 'Well, if you didn't want that sort of thing you shouldn't have come out with us.' So I said, 'Right, I'm not going out with you, it's as simple as that. QED.' Then they came around work demanding my presence to my personnel manageress, Miss Pritchard, and stood there refusing to go until she produced me. This brought a tirade onto my head about the undesirable elements I was mixing with and a comment that I wore too much make-up and Miss P was going to tell my mother! Mother would have been furious because she and the personnel manageress had this tremendous thing going between them. They used to write to each other to assure themselves of my welfare although they had only met for half an hour. Miss Pritchard was an absolute dragon. If you put her in Cell Block H, she'd look perfectly cast! She was a real warder.

Unfortunately for both of us, Miss Pritchard lived in the hostel when I moved in and I played various tricks on her. I got into trouble because Dick, who became my husband, used to play the guitar outside on the parapets at midnight to serenade me. Yet I had a champion in my immediate boss, a very handsome man of thirty-five. I instantly fell in love with him. He was totally unobtainable but he ended up giving me away at my wedding. My father refused to come because I was pregnant and he wanted to save face. My mother came and said, 'I told you you would get into this trouble,' and all the rest of it. In fact, my parents partially brought it on themselves because they told Dick and me we had to wait two years to get married. And in the hot-house environment of Earls Court, there was no way we could have held out two years. Anyway, you got no advice. It was also the testing of the wings to be independent, and although there wasn't quite a sexual revolution, a lot more people were doing it than had done before. Dick and I felt very serious about each other and we were thrown together in a bedsit quite often. He was working and had a steady job in insurance but just didn't make enough money to satisfy my parents at the time.

I can remember sort of losing my virginity, vividly. Dick was, and I can't put it really delicately, having a grope and he thought we had actually consummated the affair. He said, 'If I had more money I would ask you to marry me.' And I said, 'Why not now?' So that was how we got engaged. I really rushed it. He wanted to be a big earner before he asked me to marry him. And my parents said, 'Two years. Hazel has got to make her mark.' By that time, I had moved to Harvey Nichols. I had been told that the accounts manager was due to retire. Because I was seemingly bright, although without qualifications, it was felt that I would make a very good accounts manager and they half promised me the job. I had been silly enough to tell my parents of this, so of course they felt I was throwing away a wonderful opportunity. They were right in a way. Who knows what might have happened? But accounts couldn't have been my forte anyway as I didn't enjoy doing them.

When I was born, my dad was fifty, and in those days fifty was old. He had seen Queen Victoria when he was a child. And by the time I was a teenager, he was a pensioner. In several ways, he was a selfish man and he used to lock himself away with his own pursuits. When he retired, he wrote plays and it was a case of, 'Be quiet, Daddy's writing.' I learnt years later that he was often having a quick kip on his desk with his head in his hands, not really doing anything very constructive. He wouldn't admit he needed a sleep in the afternoons. So much of my life was 'Don't do this, your father won't like it.' I found in later years that my mother was my father's mouthpiece and that half what she said was actually what he wanted her to say, and not what she felt. I took Mother to see Bill Haley despite all the seat slashing that had gone on, according to the papers. She was jumping up and down in her seat and tapping her feet. She thought it was magic. My father couldn't believe she'd gone and had liked it. She was really quite with it. In later years, we had a lot of fun together. Mother was very into amusement arcades. I used to feed her lots of small change and her eyes would light up as she would sort of swing the one-armed bandit round and round, winning more often than not. There was a lot of fun in my mother which was held down by my father being twenty years older.

During my teens, I made some of my clothes myself and it was all done by hand. The dresses with the big skirts mostly came from C & A's. We didn't have a sewing-machine. Occasionally I would make a dress at school, but mostly it was long stitch, which is why I didn't make that many. Clothes were very important. My parents would provide my school uniform and the basic essentials, but to buy the clothes I wanted, I worked part-time.

I first worked as an assistant in an arts-cum-gift shop in Brixham. The gift shop subsidized the art supplies. Although there were lots of artists in Brixham, in the season you made a lot more money selling cheap tourist stuff. We would have these ships wheels with glass in the spokes and you would have to cut out postcards and put them underneath the glass when you were not busy. And I served lunches and cream teas in a café.

I was also an artist's model, although not *that* sort of artist's model. This artist rented a warehouse which was built into a cavern in the back of Brixham Quay. It was totally unfurbished, it was just a cave. He used to do portraits for two shillings and sixpence. To encourage people to have these portraits done, I would sit for him as if I was a total stranger and he would draw me endlessly day after day after day to get these people to sit for him. In between times I would keep the bonfire going at the back of the cavern to keep us warm because it wasn't always warm weather. I'd sweep the cave out! It was no surprise I came to get a very bad reputation because he was married. He had these little kids and he didn't get on with his wife, that sort of thing. There was never anything

going on between us. Strangely, after I moved up to Earls
Court I bumped into him. He had actually left Brixham
and had come to Earls Court, which was symptomatic of
the times. It was the most fantastic thing that in the
middle of Earls Court, there he was! And we went for a
coffee and that was it, end of story, I never saw him ever
again. He used to wear a beret and was long, thin and
starved looking which was very appropriate for his image
as an artist.

The last part-time job I did was in a photographic kiosk
on the quay at Torquay. The photographers used to take
pictures and I used to dole them out when they were
ready. The boss would come in, deliver the pictures and
take the money. It was my first feeling of independence. I
was fifteen and I ran the show, there on my own all day at
weekends and throughout the holidays as well, and it was
great. If a photograph got lost, it was my job to find it. If
people didn't like their snaps, it was my job to placate
them. It gave me my first taste of working on my own. I
also bought cigarettes out of my earnings. I started
smoking when I was thirteen or fourteen in the barn with
my buddies. Our cleaning lady told my mother and she did
her crust, saying 'I'm not going to tell you to smoke a
whole packet of twenty so that it makes you sick, because
looking at your face I think you'll do it, but I shall be very
cross if I find you doing it again.' My father smoked, not
drastically, but he did and it was the thing to do in the
Fifties. A packet of Craven A please! They didn't stop you
buying them if you were young in those days. You just
said they were for your father and they sold them to you.

My first impression of London was that it was quite
magic. It was everything I wanted and I didn't feel scared.
I felt somehow in charge, except in Putney, which was a
'no no' place – nothing happened there, and I didn't have
any money, anyway, so I couldn't really do anything.
Earls Court was a village. People knew each other and
there was a warm welcome. There was no need to be
afraid. Earls Court wasn't considered 'Town'. We used to
say we were going up to Town and would mean the West

End. That was nice, you did the sights. But you needed money. More often than not you stayed in your 'village', and it was great, the whole cosmopolitan atmosphere.

I met Dick through the crowd of people I went around with. Everyone tended to meet in the coffee bars and if you were into guitars (as I was) then you were in that group and Dick played the guitar. We used to go to The Troubadour, which is still in the same place and under the same ownership. The Kontiki, near Kensington Olympia, was another coffee bar where I used to meet friends. But The Troubadour was the main hang-out and I used to so enjoy it. Everybody gravitated to the Troubadour, in those days, by word of mouth. I remember the Viper Skiffle group – before they were well known, the lead guitarist used to go down on his own and play for his coffee and a free meal. The Troubadour had matting on the floor in the basement and if you were lucky you sat on a cushion. We stayed there for the price of a coffee, or maybe two, all evening, bearing in mind we used to not go out until half-past nine or ten o'clock, anyway. So we sat on the floor over this one or maybe two coffees if the proprietor, Mike, was lucky, listening to the skiffle or to the guitarist. It could be a different performer every night, but Johnny was down there most nights and he was the first one to give me a lighter.

Mike and his crew were doing a public service keeping us children off the streets. We had 'intellectual' conversations, all us office clerks and artists, just anybody who had anything to say. If you were homosexual, you went to the Coleherne. We didn't talk about it, though, in the Fifties. Society's attitude was ridicule and homosexuality was illegal. But it was known about, it was there. In Earls Court, the freedoms were considerably wider than in the rest of the country, especially the freedom of speech and the freedom to acknowledge that homosexuality existed. I knew nothing before I came to London except the basic facts of life. Believe it or not, I didn't learn an awful lot more. The space of time I lived there was so short. I was seventeen-and-a-half when I arrived, and knocking nineteen when I got married, so the whole scene, a whole life, encapsulated roughly twenty months. It seems longer, as all my real living was done in that time before I got married.

In some ways, I was still very much dependent upon my family. When I used to write to my mother after I came to London, I would ask her to send me up my teddy bear and things I should have taken with me and had left behind. They dutifully came up by post. At one point, I had moved from the hostel to my sister's for a while. I can't begin to think how it all happened now, but I moved back to London again and got another job and moved in with three other girls who were absolutely clique-y and excluded me. I had the smallest, coldest bedroom and it was coming up to winter. I had only one blanket because that is all I had brought up with me. I froze and desperately wrote to my mother, 'Please, I need more blankets.' I was getting quite humble by then and rather chastened at finding out what the world was really about. Of course, I did get my blankets. But there were many things that I needed which I had to go without through lack of money. There were other things I longed for of sentimental value. Suddenly, I was missing home.

I enjoyed doing my job well and liked my co-workers. I found them good fun. When I started at Derry's, we had upright desks at chest height and you perched on the stool. You had the old accounting machines and in the middle of the room all the telephones were arranged around a pillar so everybody heard what you were saying. I was terrified of using the phone to answer a query to a customer because the boss was always listening and you felt, 'Gosh, it's only been a few times I've done this, I'm going to make a fool of myself.' Everybody listened to what you were saying. If you made a mistake, it was self-evident right from the start. And the boss used to come out to make sure nobody was talking. He had a vast cubicle in the corner and was always peering out through the glass. About six times a day he would come out of his cubicle and pace up and down with his hands behind his back, watching us all to make sure that we weren't talking, that we weren't eating, that we weren't doing anything we shouldn't be doing. It was very antiquarian. You thought of *The Christmas Carol*. It was also very much like school, hence Miss Pritchard's interference and also my boss telling her, 'Mind your own business, she's a good worker, I don't want to lose her.' That was the saving of me. He was wonderful, that man.

I used to think that most of the girls I worked with were pretty in their different ways. There was much much less of the influence of clothes on things in those days. We were very much all in the same boat. We weren't affluent, we didn't mix in affluent circles. There wasn't this overlapping of the 'haves' and 'have nots', or the groping upwards that people do nowadays. We were much more content with what we had. We felt that possibly if we worked hard and did well, we, too, would enjoy the fruits. Life was pretty good. A cup of coffee in the Troubadour was as good as a night out on the town.

We went to films, too. I can remember *Oklahoma*, and I always loved Sophia Loren. She was the epitome of what I wanted to be – feminine. She never lost any of her femininity and I suppose I saw her in *Boy on a Dolphin* and never forgot it. She was so beautiful and has always remained that way for me. And Margaret Lockwood and James Mason! With James Mason, it was his voice and slight manly dominance I always appreciated. Although I am independent, now, I still prefer men to be dominant in some ways. I suppose that was my upbringing. I like a man to be 'a man'. I still like doors to be held open for me! That doesn't mean to say that I can't hold doors open for somebody who is more feeble or whatever than me. It works like that for me. But James Mason thrilled me because he frightened me slightly in some of the films. He had just a touch of evil.

When I got married, it was with due pomp and ceremony except that my father wasn't there. This was 1957 and I was eighteen-and-a-half. Dick was a Catholic and I went through all the instruction to see whether I should change my religion. Then they said to us, 'Of course you realize that if you are having a baby, and it is a question of the baby's life or the mother's, we will expect your husband to save the baby's life.' We were both horrified and I said, 'Come on, if I survive, I would probably be capable of having half a dozen kids. It is not logical.'

We were married in Fulham Palace Road – the Servite Church, St Phillip Neri – and it was a Priory. The funny thing was we were living in digs in Tregunter Road and one day the Father came round to see us to talk about the last-minute preparations. One of the other lodgers answered the door. There stands this monk in a habit with a tonsure, and he says, 'I am Prior Tuck' and the guy said, 'You are kidding, you have got to be joking.' 'No, no, I am Prior Tuck. I have come to see Mr Alton and Miss Hayward.' They wouldn't believe him, they wouldn't let him in. They thought it was some kind of belated April Fool's joke! Eventually, he did manage to convince them he was genuine but we weren't in anyway. Can you imagine? He was actually Prior Tuck.

When I went to file for divorce, I applied for legal aid. Although we lived in Surrey, the office they sent me to for the legal aid papers was next door to the church I married in. That was the biggest body blow that I could have had over the divorce. Life has been full of coincidences like that. But I lovingly made my own wedding dress, finishing it the night before my marriage at two o'clock in the morning.

I don't know what I thought marriage was going to be like. All I can remember is that I was upset because I poured make-up down the front of my wedding dress. I had to stick a carnation on the front, which I hadn't planned to do, to cover the spot. It was a nice wedding for twenty-five pounds. I didn't really enjoy the sex. I used to wonder, 'Is that all it's about?' I think that's what the marriage really foundered on because my husband couldn't talk to me about it. When I belatedly and desperately went to the Marriage Guidance Council, they wrote to him asking him to come in and give his side of the story.

He tore up the letter and said: 'Bloody voyeurs.' So that was the end. Of course when the sexual revolution started to take place and I read in the papers and magazines about what was supposed to be happening, I realized what had been missing. It also seemed to me that every time we did it, I got pregnant. It wasn't until I divorced that I knew really what had been going wrong. My husband told me years later that if he had gone to the Marriage Guidance Council he would have had to acknowledge there were problems and he didn't know how to deal with that. He was frightened he might find out things about me he wouldn't want to know, like maybe I had been unfaithful to him. But that is another story.

During the Fifties, I think the things I was most attached to were things I made myself, the things I was proud to have done. Mostly these were clothes, but I also wrote poetry. Just before I left home, my mother found one poem I had written called 'The Eternal Triangle'. It was about a love affair. Strangely, it was a love affair that came out all right because the woman stayed with her husband. My mother was horrified. The sex was insinuation only, nothing specific and nothing rude about it. In fact my ex-husband found it shortly after we agreed to part. He, very naughtily I suspect, had been going through my things. He was in tears and brought it to me, saying: 'You should have this published.' I had waited twenty-four years for that particular bit of praise because my parents never praised anything I did. Whatever I did, both my father and mother used to say, 'Very nice, dear, but if I were you I would have done so and so' or 'You could have done better' or 'What a pity you didn't get six O-levels instead of five'. With the money they had spent on me with private tuition, they expected more.

Dick and I found it difficult to find accommodation at the time of our marriage because I was pregnant and nobody in London would take children. We had to move out to Sussex and we paid two pounds a week rent. Dick earned eight pounds. Of that, he had to spend almost two running the motorbike to the station and taking the train into the City. We were very hard up. It is extraordinary to think that when I had Solange, I took her with me straw-berry- and gooseberry-picking in order to make ends meet. It was hard back-breaking work. I might come home with huge amounts of strawberries, but we were only allowed the bird-pecked ones. I'd cut the bad bits out. We pigged out on strawberries for weeks. Of course, there were no freezers then. We had a hundred pounds as a wedding present from my father and had we had the proper advice, we would have put it as a deposit on a house. We wouldn't have had to move out of London at all. But nobody assisted. In the Fifties, you very much did everything yourself, particularly if you got married under our circum-stances. Three years later, when we did put a down-payment on a house, it was exactly one hundred pounds.

We didn't have a honeymoon when we got married as we only had ten bob between us. Dick went to work as usual on the Monday and we lived on bread and scrape for a week. We didn't feel deprived, though. This was strange considering I came from a relatively well-off family. It was more par for the course for Dick. To hear him talk, now, they had newspaper on the table which was changed once a week, a bucket in the corner of the bedroom and an outside loo. Part of this is true, but I was from better circumstances. However, we were used to Bedsitland and accustomed to Rachmanism and the things that went on, so if we had to move to Sussex to have our child, so be it.

I worked at a local sawmill until I was five months' pregnant. Women didn't let on they were expecting and no one at work would know until it became rather obvious. So I worked in this sawmill with a lot of guys. When I was definitely showing, the boss came to me and said: 'We are sorry but you've got to go, we don't need to tell you why.' That was it. I wasn't told I was entitled to a pregnancy allowance so I never got that. After I had Solange, I found out that I should have had this weekly payment. I couldn't claim it retrospectively so I lost it completely. We were desperate for the money.

Our rented home was a mews cottage which was damp,

cold and extremely 'cottagey'. Nowadays, people wouldn't tolerate the conditions. For heating, there was only a single-bar electric fire, or we burned wood. The larder, which led off the kitchen, had galvanized iron wire with holes in it so when you opened the larder door, you got blown backwards and the snow used to filter through. We had one of these stoves with legs on and this was 1957! It was grey enamel with a white door, the type that went out in the Forties. We had an immersion heater and the electricity bill crippled us. And so, we lived above our income to the tune of something like one pound, fifty pence a week. This is a disaster when you took home only eight pounds.

The bathroom was hysterical. We had an old stone sink and a huge cast-iron bath twice the size of anything you see now. I disappeared in it and it was very difficult to get the hot water to stay hot. On the floor, there was blue linoleum paint, like they used on ship's decks, and draughts through the floorboards. I suppose we had two changes of sheets and five or six towels as wedding presents and they stayed with us for years. It wasn't a bad life but it was hard. It was what you expected. Most young people who got married at that age were in the same situation. It was our fault that we married young, although everybody was doing it. Sadly, it was impossible to keep up with the friends I had made in London. There wasn't the means to do it. We didn't have a phone until very much later and then it was strictly for emergencies. The friends I had made in the hostel had gone their different ways, anyway, and we all lost touch.

In the meantime, Dick caught flu, I nursed Dick and caught pneumonia. Being pregnant, I was rushed into hospital. When it came to deciding what to do about having Solange, I flatly refused to go into hospital again. Despite the fact it was my first birth, I had my baby at home. It was April and the weather was getting better. I told the doctor not to attend but he turned up, anyway, and I was furious because he laughed all the way through. I had a midwife too. It was a natural birth with no problems.

There was no help after I had my baby. The midwife came for a few weeks and then I was on my own. It was the sort of village where the doctor came once a week. I suppose there must have been an emergency service of some sort but nothing really went wrong. I coped. I didn't rely on anybody except myself. For the first baby, there wasn't any child allowance. You had a maternity grant and then eight shillings a week for the second baby. I had Justine fifteen months later. We were desperately trying to make ends meet. Dick used to go and clean an office before he went to work at his nine to five job and then clean a further two offices in the evening. He did three nights a week teaching guitar at night school. Most nights he wasn't home until ten or eleven. On Friday, after work, he went drinking with the lads and caught the last train, so he might be home at one a.m. I understood his need to do this because he did all these jobs. One night a week with the boys was no problem as far as I was concerned.

But you have to also look at it from my point of view. Our radio broke, there was no television, there was no washing-machine, no freezer, no fridge, no vacuum cleaner. I swept the house, and it took me an hour-and-a-half each day to do the washing by hand assisted by an electric boiler. That's why, I think, I am so house-proud now. I got used to doing these things, got used to being ultra-clean, because there was nothing else to do. I had no friends. I went to the Young Wives' Club but they were all rather 'County' and I didn't fit in with them as I was only nineteen. They were tolerant of me, though. The Clubs were always in the afternoons so I was very much on my own at night. I did a lot of sewing and knitting. When Dick was home, he played the guitar and we would go for walks. That was our only entertainment other than our child. I don't remember being unhappy at all or dissatisfied. To a certain extent perhaps that might have been will power – I made the best of what I had because that was the way life was. We expected that what we got was the result of our own efforts. We expected things would eventually change

– if we didn't, we would have gone crazy. I certainly would have gone stir crazy.

It was seven miles to the nearest town and I had to bus or walk everywhere. There was a village shop, but it was expensive. I would often walk to the next village three miles away to save the bus fare into Haywards Heath but we rarely went into town. The advantage of the village shop was that you had all your groceries and meat and fish delivered as well as your milk. I could take a set order to the shop and they would bring it. But this rather isolated me as well. I said that I didn't have the contact with other young mothers, really with anybody at all. There was no clinic, the midwife came to see me. There was not a great sense of community in that particular village. Everyone was a bit conservative, snobby and 'True Blue', and if you didn't fit that particular description, they didn't bother much with you. My inclination, at the time, was to be like them but we didn't fit because we didn't have any money. And the villagers at the other end of the social strata didn't want to know us either – we belonged with the establishment but we hadn't made it yet.

I had a very touching faith in Dick because he assured me he would do well. When you think about it, this man of twenty-one, suddenly landed with a wife and a child, is assuring his teenage bride that life will be a bed of roses in the future. That ambition, to be fair to him, has carried on right through his life, that feeling that he is in control. Occasionally he may have faltered but he never ever (until much later on) had any doubts about where we were going and what he was going to do for his wife and what were, eventually, three children in very quick succession. If I had to be in my situation, he was probably the best person to have been married to. I did try birth control and it didn't work for me. There was nothing as foolproof as the Pill. And so, it was fifteen months between my first two children and thirteen months between the second two.

When I was pregnant, I wore home-made smocks and skirts with huge 'U'-fronts cut out of them, absolutely diabolical. I also had an enormous ugly pair of corduroy trousers with expandable hooks – which looked a bit like a separator – and ribbons. So I had three smocks, the trousers and one skirt, and I looked dreadful. One of the smocks was turquoise with no sleeves, rickrack braid and white spots. The clothes were awful but that was maternity fashion and there wasn't much choice. I didn't have a sewing-machine and besides, I didn't have the energy, given the time at my disposal between getting married and really advanced pregnancy. It wasn't really worth sewing clothes the way I used to. Later on, with my second child, I had access to a sewing-machine and made some nicer things.

Dick was in the habit of trying to trap things for meat for our table. He hid it from me that he had actually killed a neighbour's cat, a lovely cat. Our neighbour came to me and said, 'We've lost our cat. If you see it, let us know.' It wasn't until 1981 when I went to work with Dick that he confessed he had snared that cat by mistake. It got into a rabbit snare he had set. He never caught a rabbit, though, so he wasn't very successful. Before coming up to London and working in the City, he had worked on a farm.

When I got married, I already knew how to cook from watching my mother. We were taught properly at school as well, although I knew most of what they taught us from home. I found domestic science boring for that reason. I wasn't conscious of being taught to cook by my mother. I had an interest in what she did and would automatically gravitate towards it. One secret she kept to herself was the magic of the 'clicking rolling-pin'. Every time she rolled pastry, the rolling-pin went 'click click' and I couldn't make it do it. My mother wouldn't tell me why the rolling-pin made this noise for her and didn't for me. I must have been very small when I first asked, but she always kept it a secret. This was her magic. I discovered when I married that the 'click click' sound was made by her wedding ring on the rolling-pin. The significance of the first time I made pastry after I married Dick was quite startling. The rolling-pin now clicked for me when I began rolling out the pastry.

# ODILE

In my mind Harold Macmillan was prime minister throughout the whole of the Fifties, but of course that wasn't true. He wasn't prime minister until 1957. I don't really start slotting events into place until the late Fifties and I don't remember Anthony Eden at all. I think the first political thing I can remember happening was some trouble over something called Suez and I hadn't a clue what that was all about. When I think of Suez I just think of the bedroom I slept in at the time in our flat in South Manchester. So if people say Suez, I think, 'I used to lie in bed and worry about "Suez" but I hadn't a clue what Suez was!' It wasn't until the Seventies when I was in my twenties that I began to have some kind of inkling of the Suez Affair.

My mother learned to drive in 1956, at the time of the Suez crisis, and that was a much bigger event. My parents had a bakery and neither of them could drive. My father used to deliver bread on this enormous grocer's bicycle with a huge basket on the front. He used to deliver bread in Stockport which was quite near to where we lived, although we actually lived in Manchester. Stockport has these enormous hills. I mean really, really steep hills. He used to go up and down the hills on his bike with this bread! I never saw him do it, but I heard stories from people who had, and I did see him setting off on the bike all loaded up. He was very fit. He still is. It's the way he is built.

But we very quickly had to have a van, so we bought this van and hired a driver. They hired this ancient-looking guy, I can remember to this day. He looked like he had one foot in the grave. I don't think he could have been so old but he had grey hair. As he was always getting ill, out came the bike again and eventually my parents decided that one of them had to learn to drive. This was the great ongoing topic, learning to drive. I thought it was

really exciting. All this was going on at the time of Suez.
My mother suddenly started driving the van. And she was
driving around on her own. It never dawned on me until I
learned to drive that of course you can't normally drive on
your own until you've got a full licence. But my mother
could. For some extraordinary reason at that time, you
didn't have to have somebody with you in the car when
you were learning. I don't know why – perhaps it was
something to do with petrol rationing? I wouldn't have
thought that two people in a car could have used any more
petrol than one person. But anyway my mother was
driving this huge van round Manchester loaded up with
bread without a proper driving licence.

The original van didn't have anything written on it – we
never had our name on the side of the van. First we had a
grotty old van and then we got a nice Bedford van, which I
thought was wonderful. Every two years we got another
van and we used to upgrade every time. Finally, we got
one with seats in the back as well, and I thought we were
really swish, because we were able to go off on camping
holidays in it. We were hopeless at camping! We were no
good putting up tents or anything practical like that, and I
used to hate it, except my mother was a whizz at cooking
over a fire but I didn't appreciate that at the time. Even
then, I always wanted to go to restaurants. I hate camping
to this day. When anyone suggests camping I think: you
must be joking! I have these childhood memories of our
attempts at having cheap camping holidays, and it was
mad. We went to Wales once – it was bloody awful. We
also went to the Isle of Wight, but that was much later.
The first trip we ever did, though, was to France. France
was actually much better for camping than this country.
The sites were always much more developed there. I know
a lot of people think camping there is not like the real
thing, because French campsites have swimming pools
and restaurants, but as a child that was exactly what I
thought was necessary for good camping. This was right
towards the end of the Fifties.

Our bakery was in South Manchester, quite near the

borders of Stockport, where eventually we went to live. My father was actually trained as a baker in France. It was an enormous bakery and we lived in the flat above it for a while. Then my mother opened the shop at the front and became a shopkeeper. That must have been in 1954. Before that, we had lived close to central Manchester for a long time, in fact from when I was born in 1950. I was born in Crumpsall Hospital, which I don't remember, but I do remember that house. It was a semi-detached house, quite an ordinary one, and it had a huge garden with lots of waving grass and a swing. I remember the grass being really long. We didn't have a lawn-mower, because we couldn't afford it, I presume. My mother used to cut the grass with scissors every so often. Well, first we had scissors and then my mother got hold of these shears, though I don't remember her actually cutting it. I remember, once, my father coming back from the bakery in the early morning and us walking through the long grass and him putting my brother and I on the swing and swinging us there and back.

That house seemed quite a big house. My mother had a washing-machine that had an electric ringer which I thought was really posh. In fact, it was a big hefty old thing. And the kitchen had a rack on the ceiling for hanging clothes. I remember orange juice and cod-liver oil coming from what we called 'The Welfare', which, of course, was the children's health supplement provided by the Government. I used to love it. I went to a nursery school that was attached to the local church. But it was a very Jewish area and half the kids were Jewish, so we used to have all the Jewish holidays and all the Christian holidays, too. That was a really good deal. We just used to play all day. I was stung by a bee once. I screamed and screamed. They rushed me to the clinic and got the sting out and I was sent home. We wore aprons at the nursery. Mine was blue with a pink duck on it. I've got photos of me wearing it in the nursery playroom. I remember that room very well.

Everything seemed very regimented in the Fifties: the

way one did things. And the overall drabness of everything: everything seemed grey when I was a child. I feel it
was a lot greyer than the Sixties, but I am not sure
whether that was because I was getting older by then and
felt differently about things.

When I was about four, we moved to live above the
bakery that I was talking about before. My father had
bought the bakery earlier and used to commute there from
our house. Eventually we went to live in the flat above it.
There were lots of terraced houses around there, you
know, two-up two-downs with back entries in alleyways. It
seemed very drab and grey. It was a world so full of 'Thou
shalt' and 'Thou shalt not'. When I think back to it, I see
the typical Fifties mentality as 'There is a right way to live
and a wrong way to live'; you know, all 'black' and 'white',
although my parents never quite seemed to fit into that.

My father is a bit of a non-conformist. He comes from a
Continental Jewish background and is very Continental in
his manner and attitudes. I always thought he would have
been happier going back to France and living there rather
than staying in this country. He really doesn't fit in with
English society. My mother also comes from a Jewish
background but she is much more British. She was born
here and her mother was born here, but her father wasn't.
Her sister, my aunt, is very much the gushing Jewish
matron that my grandmother was, but my mother isn't
like that. She is much quieter and seems to fit in naturally
with what I think of as English society – all that my father
and my home background didn't fully slot into at all.

My father's family were Eastern European – Polish –
well, the bit where the borders of Poland are these days,
somewhere in Russia or Czechoslovakia. It all used to
change every five minutes. When he was three years old,
his family went to live in France and he grew up in Nancy
in north eastern France, which had a large Polish–Jewish
community. Probably if it hadn't been for Hitler, the
Nazis and the Second World War, he would have stayed
there. My mother's family also came from Eastern Europe
– the Ukraine – sometime in the 1850s, and they got as far

as Liverpool. My grandmother was an orthodox Jew but we weren't brought up that way.

When I was about six, my parents decided that I should at least know something about Judaism. There are a whole procession of Jewish holidays that take place in September and we generally went to synagogue for that little grouping. My parents aren't really the slightest bit religious. We never had the Friday night Shabbat until my grandmother came to live with us. She always lit the candles on Friday night. I used to be watching TV while she did it. We even ate bacon butties when she wasn't around!

My father is really an atheist. I wanted to become a Catholic at one point in my life and he said, 'Why do that? Why trade one religion for another?' Religion, as far as my father is concerned, is the fodder of the masses and he told me that from the age of five, before I could really know what he meant. He was a card-carrying member of the Communist Party when he was young and was arrested in France for taking part in various political activities. But his father was a cantor in the synagogue and my grandmother's father on my mother's side was a rabbi. Of my father's family, only my father and his brother, Joseph, survived the War.

I didn't really feel Jewish at all. My mother's attitude towards religion was that she was born Jewish but she had no real interest. My parents and their generation were part of the Thirties' great left-wing atheistic movement. As a child, I was confused by the Judaism. On the one hand, my parents were saying I ought to know something about the religious background I came from, but God and religion didn't come into our everyday life at all. My parents actually told me that they didn't believe in God. It is not surprising with this background that I always thought I was very different from the other kids at school. The things we did, the way we ate, all seemed to be something else. I saw the contrasts when I went to my school friends' houses. The other school kids didn't have a big meal in the evening. I always thought other people didn't have enough to eat! The English always seemed to eat bits of bread and butter and were always prim and proper! We always ate more and we always seemed to eat nicer things. A lot of what people call delicatessen food now, we were eating as the norm then with this Jewish background. I certainly didn't like the English food at all, when I had tea at a friend's house. All over England, it seemed to me, the evening meal was high tea – bread and butter and jam – with egg and bacon if you were lucky. I thought, 'What is this? These people don't eat at all.' We had a proper dinner, but we usually called it tea, a Northern term for your evening meal. In the North, dinner is what you have at lunchtime and tea is what you have in the evening. Everyone else seemed to have horrible nasty white bread while, of course, we had the nice Continental bread from our bakery.

We also had a midday meal at school, which I didn't like. It used to make me sick. Often it would be stewed meat with gristle and fat and to this day the one kind of food I cannot eat is stewed meat. It reminds me of school food and makes me want to throw up on the table! I couldn't stand the very, very overcooked Jewish food either. My mother used to make chicken soup and kneidlich balls until they came out of our ears. Actually, I loved them.

Manchester just seemed very drab, though our neighbourhood wasn't a particularly poor area. It was residential, and it wasn't the real endless back-to-backs of the worst parts of Manchester, it was in-between, lower-middle/upper-working class, though people didn't have a lot of money. There was some council housing, but not council housing as we think of it from the Sixties. Some of it was quite desirable. I am sure, now, these houses are being bought up and the whole area is changing, being 'yuppified', if you like. It just seemed, then, as if money was tight and luxury goods were non-existent. I suppose as children we didn't really think about money, but we boasted 'My dad's got a car', or 'Well, we've got a van'. I don't think my parents would have had a van if we hadn't run a bakery. We didn't even get a television until 1958, when I was eight.

But before that, when I was seven, we moved again, nearer the centre of Manchester, into a flat above another shop we had bought. We kept the bakery on with the first shop and my mother ran a little delicatessen at the new shop. I went to a nearby school, which was in the park. It was not an open-air school but it was built with large verandahs around a green. The classroom windows opened out onto the verandahs all the way around this green. It wasn't the usual old Victorian school, like the first one I'd been to.

I didn't really fit in at school. I always felt I was a bit weird and a bit different. We didn't have to wear a uniform, but we had to wear neat skirts and socks. You know, girls were girls and boys were boys. I had long hair which was tied, for neatness, in two bows at either side. I hated school as I hated being disciplined and being told what to do. I hated going out on cold mornings and being told it was good for me. I thought this was ridiculous and I wasn't going to do it! My mother had a lot of trouble with me and school. I was bullied at school and I didn't like to take the Jewish holidays because no one else did and I didn't want to feel too different. I also had a mentally handicapped brother and would have to explain to people what was wrong with him. I found that very difficult. I wanted to fit in.

Everything was much more closed-in then. Near this second school in the park, part of the neighbourhood was even more working class than where we had lived before. There were more of the small back-to-back terraced houses that you used to see in Manchester and I remember kids at that school who I thought were really rough and really scruffy. Some didn't even have bathrooms in their houses. You very rarely get that now but in the Fifties there was an awful lot of it in Manchester. I was told that these children bathed at the swimming baths – they actually had baths for taking a bath in there, then. I knew there were these baths, because when we used to go to the swimming pool we'd see the sign pointing to them.

I suppose we were living in working-class neighbour-hoods, and, in a way, we were working class too, only we owned a business. A lot of the fathers of the kids around us were unskilled workers. They didn't seem to have any particular trade. I think there was a fair amount of work around, at least I assume so. I didn't know anybody who was out of work. There were always jobs on the buses, or you could be a milkman.

Everyone I came in contact with was white. The first black person I saw was when I was four and I was fascin-ated by him. I remember seeing him across the street. The only black people I had seen before were on films, Tarzan films, and they would come out of the jungle going 'Woooooo' and waving spears at you. I was really fascin-ated to see this man wearing ordinary clothes and not coming to attack me with a spear. There were no black children at school until I was in the secondary school, in the Sixties, and even then there were very few. Once my grandmother brought me back a black doll from South Africa. It was dressed as a Zulu warrior, but I didn't know that. Because it was wearing a skirt – even though it was a fur skirt – I thought it must be a 'girl' doll, so I called it Topsy. Over the years, Topsy lost all her African gear and became a black doll dressed in a white baby outfit. I got it all wrong. I now realize the doll was dressed as a Zulu warrior. I just got it all wrong.

I really enjoyed dressing up, although I thought women were very strange. I noticed when I was getting towards about eight or nine that women had these enormous pointed breasts. Of course, an awful lot of that was the bras they wore in the Fifties. I'm sure that not everybody would have had enormous pointed breasts even with those bras (!), but I was very worried that I would have enor-mous tits like that and I would find it very difficult to move around. I was also more than worried about the fact that one minute you seemed to have this body that was quite normal and moved in all directions and, suddenly, as you approached being a woman, you had to bind it in and wear awful shoes you couldn't walk in, and stockings and suspenders. I just thought 'Yuck'! It wasn't that you wore make-up to look nice, you had to wear make-up or else you weren't a woman. There was this awful attitude. I thought I was going to have to go through all this and I was really dreading it. Of course, when I got to the right age the mini skirt had just started to arrive and you didn't have all this funny underwear. Fashion had changed. I was just so relieved, as from the age of about eight I'd been worrying about this peculiar creature I would have to become. I could not imagine what was going to happen to me to make me like that.

I was fascinated by Princess Anne because she was exactly the same age as me. There were pictures of her dresses in lots of comics and magazines. I ended up having quite a few dresses like hers. Sometimes I really wanted them and some of the chain stores like Marks & Spencer would even sell what they called 'Princess' dresses. The regimented costume for a party was a fluffy net white dress and an angora cardigan. I had a whole series of them. I also had long hair, most of the time, as a child. My mother tried to curl it. She never got as far as a perm, but she did curl it with rollers. For a while it was also cut short.

My mother wasn't someone who thought, 'Here's my little girl, she's got to do this that and the other.' She's not a dictatorial person. My grandmother was more like that. But my mother would sometimes look at me and think 'Ah, we're going somewhere nice, make Odile look nice.' My mother is quite conventional in a way, she would dress in conventional clothes. I also wanted conventional things, then, because I felt such an oddball at school with my big nose and my Jewish background and my mentally retarded brother, and I wanted to fit, somehow. Princess Anne may have a prominent nose, but she also was golden-haired and seemed a much prettier little girl than me. I wanted to fit in and be one of the gang, though at the same time, I didn't want to fit in because I resented the other kids for making me feel I was so different from them.

As my parents were better off than many of the people who lived around us, my mother generally dressed me a little bit nicer than most, getting things specially made. These clothes were of good quality. She also knew somebody who had a knitting-machine and made these lovely little skirts for me. I really liked them. I remember somebody, near where my parents had the shop, making me a little trouser suit towards the end of the Fifties. Sometimes I used to be very shy of taking my coat off. I was very proud of my clothes, but at the same time I felt I wouldn't be one of the gang if I turned out in these slightly better outfits. My mother didn't buy me many chain-store outfits and I sometimes wanted them so much. Occasionally, I would be allowed one or two. Marks & Spencer is where we got a lot of these clothes and they were often quite nice cotton. I remember having a very nice blue dress from M & S, which I really liked. There are photos of me in it. Also, there was this very popular flower skirt that M & S did around 1958 with roses on, in either pink or yellow. I wanted one but I got the yellow and everyone else had it in pink. I was so pleased that mine was slightly different, but at the same time I felt slightly out of it. Marks & Spencer only did clothes then, no food or other things. Green and gold, those were the two trademark colours of M & S then, and they remained so until quite recently. Their nearest big store to us was in central Manchester and we used to go there quite often.

My mother has naturally curly hair. It's frizzy and she used to hate it, because although you would think it fitted in with the Fifties Look, being curly, Fifties hair was also shaped in a particular way. Hers was just naturally frizzy, and she could never get the exact style she wanted to stay in. She would go to the hairdresser once a week, to get her to try and tame it a bit, and then not wash it in between! A lot of women of her generation still go to the hairdresser once a week. But this used to be normal and I used to think, 'Oh, God, I can't face having to do this, either.' It all seemed so difficult, what was expected of you as a woman. I was approaching the end of the Fifties, determined that I would become a tomboy. I was really firm about that. A lot of girls couldn't wait to get into all the fashions and things, but I didn't want to know.

There was also the business of sex and all that. In my mother's shop, I used to see these boxes come in with 'Sanitary Towels' on the side. Now, I knew what a towel was, and I knew what the word 'sanitary' meant, and I thought: well, why should a towel be sanitary? Or why shouldn't *all* towels be sanitary rather than buying special sanitary towels? I was never aware that women had periods until I was about ten, when I finally had to ask. I was also given a book about sex, but I didn't really equate it with periods. It was about fruit flies, this book. These fruit flies were mating and it was all about genes and chromosomes but was nothing to do with how they did it.

I didn't think anything much, then, of the opposite sex, although I was bullied by boys at school and I didn't really like most of them. I did have crushes on odd boys, though. One of the boys I fancied, I actually sat next to for a while in class. I would love to know what he looks like, now, because I still have a clear memory of him, and there was no doubt that he was the hero of the class; really handsome. I remember him between the ages of nine and ten. He was called Charles. Imagine, he came from an ordinary working-class family, and they had called him Charles. That was really unusual. It made us laugh. He was extremely good-looking and I imagine he must still be. He had a lightly tanned skin with a few freckles over his nose, bright blue eyes, and this wave of blond hair. Everybody – whether they liked him or not – thought he was extremely handsome. He knew he was special, but when you got to know him he was also quite nice. We had a grading system to prepare for the eleven-plus exam and we were divided into four groups. The kids who sat at the back of the class were the top of their group and the dumbos were at the front. I was sort of in between. When I did very badly, I was moved towards the front and finally, quite by chance, because I had done so badly on one test, I got to sit next to Charles for two months.

Everybody in the class teased me about it. I think they might have been jealous but I thought, me, sitting next to Charles and I'm the ugliest girl in the class. I was convinced I was the ugliest girl in the world because I wasn't pretty in the English pretty-pretty sense of the word. A pretty girl had blonde sandy hair and blue eyes and clipped little features. That was the Fifties ideal, in my eyes. I had a pale skin and a long nose, and I just wasn't this Fifties creature. They always used to call me 'Big Nose'. So to sit next to Charles was absolutely wonderful, and the kids used to take the rise out of me about it. And then we got different grades in our exams and I moved away from him.

Our last two years at junior school were totally devoted towards getting through the eleven-plus exam. You felt that your whole life depended on it, because if you didn't pass it and go to grammar school, you probably wouldn't take any GCEs. I didn't really know what a GCE was, then, but I knew no GCEs could mean you wouldn't escape from your background and have a good job. I'm sure in some households it didn't matter. In the household I came from it was very important to do well. Richard, my husband, comes from a lower-middle-class background and his parents obviously took a very active role in his education. My parents didn't to quite the same extent and I wouldn't say that they really pressurized me, but it is almost part of the atmosphere in a Jewish household that you wouldn't want to stay where you are. The hope is that you will move up. My parents weren't nasty about it, they were very sympathetic, but it was something you felt you had to do.

I didn't get on very well at school in the early years. I had difficulty learning to read and I had tremendous problems doing some of the expected things. I was very good at maths, but I had problems doing exams. Serious problems of actually sitting there and doing them, nothing to do with nerves. I failed my eleven-plus examination. I just sat there and couldn't be bothered to do anything. I could probably have answered the paper quite easily, but I just spent a lot of time staring out of the window. My results didn't come out for quite a long time, because I transferred counties. My mother finally went down to the education office to sort it out. They found my results and told her I'd failed. She then asked if I'd at least done well enough to be in a GCE stream at the secondary modern school, and they said, 'No, actually, we'd be very surprised if a girl with results like this could get a GCE at all.'

I spent two years in a secondary-modern school. I just don't like any kind of regimented situation and that's what school and exams seemed like to me. As a child I couldn't fit around them or learn to play the game. It was not until I was getting on twelve or thirteen, when I transferred to a grammar school, that I started to, somehow. I began to do quite well in exams; maybe because I just decided to do them, having been put in that situation. I think I suddenly realized I had the chance to do GCEs, a chance to escape my background, which is what I thought I had to do. I just didn't want to be working class, grafting for a living. I didn't want to have a business, either, like my parents, because I thought that was grafting for a living, as well. I wanted to become a professional. My uncle in London, who was the pride of the family, had been to Oxford and he was a professional. He ended up in films, on the executive side. I think he was quite important at one time. These days I have mixed feelings about him. I think he is quite conventional and not really a very interesting person. In his own field he probably did do well, though he's not really someone I can identify with. But for a long time I thought I should be an achiever in the kind of way he was.

Once I started to do well at school, my parents wanted me to become a doctor or lawyer, a very Jewish thing. I thought I wanted to be a doctor, too, for an awfully long time, until I realized it wasn't me at all. I spent a lot of my teens, in fact way into my twenties, fighting the guilt about not doing medicine, and going back and doing courses, trying to conform and fit in with this role. I wish I had never had that guilt loaded onto me. I think I might have achieved a lot more earlier. It is only in the years since my early thirties that I have broken away from it, and it is only in the last two years that I really don't care any more and have no guilt about it whatsoever. This emphasis on achievement also seems a particularly Fifties thing, for someone who comes from the kind of background I did. Mine is the first educated generation. I know my uncle went to Oxford back in the Thirties, but he was an exception in our family. The majority of our family was still in that upper-working-class/lower-middle-class bracket. Mine was the first generation to have an opportunity to get a bit better education, to go to university *en masse*. All the family, from my generation upwards, have had higher education and are solidly middle class. There is no question about it. Even though two of my cousins didn't go to university, they became solidly middle class in some other way. Up until us, there just wasn't the opportunity. There was this promised land after the War, hopes of a better and more equal future. It was going to happen, but it didn't emerge straight away and we were the children of those post-war years, the ones who eventually got all the benefits. There was this great atmosphere of 'Get your eleven-plus examination and get on in life!' It was just so important. So much of our early school was just about getting into grammar school and passing our exams, so we could get on. Although I don't think every child in the Sixties had a more relaxed attitude hoisted onto them, I am sure that there was a much freer attitude towards this exam-oriented achievement.

I hated school. I get up in the morning for work these days and I say to Richard, 'I'm off to "school" now.' We call it 'school', both of us, and we both hate it, but Richard is someone who is more able to conform than I am. He hates it but he can just smile and get on with it. His parents have very much got this Fifties post-war mentality. They are the same generation as my parents and have the same kind of mentality and attitude towards things. Richard was shuffled off to a boys' public school instead of the local comprehensive school, which meant a heavy academic atmosphere, just like the high school I went to.

As I became more educated, my father shied away from me. He felt I was ashamed of him because he had no education, he was just an old baker and he used to wear overalls. He wanted me to have a good education, but he became jealous of it and thought my mother pushed me away from him. My mother had been a secretary when they got married. Then she was a housewife before she helped out in the bakery, finally opening the shops. I liked all the different things in the shops but I also hated the idea of them because it meant there was always work for her to do and I didn't see much of her. I got it into my head very young: You want to get out of this, you want to have a better life. You get an education. You get an education and become middle class. No businesses, no working Sundays, no working Saturdays. You should have a good life. So I thought education and education alone was the key to a good life, which is a load of old bullshit. It really put me off doing anything enterprising for years and years.

My parents weren't around very much when I was growing up. They always seemed busy with business. We had cleaning ladies to look after us, who would pick us up from school and bring us home. When we lived at the back of one of the shops, we saw my parents on and off in little bits with them flitting in and out of the flat, but we didn't get constant attention. When we moved into a separate house with a garden, and so on, I thought it was great. I thought we were really going up in the world, but the cleaning lady was still looking after us.

I got pocket money. There was a little savings bank at school which we put money into and I was very proud of this. I also had a post office savings account and I was really anxious to get it up to the one-hundred-pound level, so I could be rich. Although my parents sold sweets in the shop, I didn't waste my money on them. Actually I wasn't keen on sweets. I loved crisps and savoury things. My mother had to explain to people who bought presents for

us that Odile didn't like sweets. My parents were very
kind and would do anything for me. They were very
loving, but I always found them distant. They were totally
lacking in understanding about what I was doing. I
suppose they were too busy making a living.

After the War, my grandmother moved with her elder
daughter to South Africa. By the late Fifties, as apartheid
and the troubles were getting worse, this daughter and her
family were thinking of leaving and didn't want to come
back to England. They emigrated to Australia and are still
there. A lot of people went to Australia in the Fifties on the
assisted-passage deal, although my relatives didn't go that
way from South Africa. But my grandmother didn't want
to do this. She just decided to come back to England and
moved in with us and stayed for ever. Granny died when I
was twenty-four. I had constant battles with her over her
whole attitude as to how girls should be brought up and
the way I should be treated. She was just a domineering
type and that was the bottom line. My mother is a bit of a
soft touch and she was domineered as well. One evening –
this was way into the Sixties – we heard a commotion
downstairs and looked over the bannister into the hallway.
My mother had come home from something rather late
and my grandmother was marching up and down the hall
saying, 'Sarah, where have you *been*?' 'Mother, I'm fifty-
odd years old, what do you mean, where have I been? I've
been out!' 'I get worried about you coming in at this time.'
This was about half past eleven, it wasn't three o'clock in
the morning! But that was my grandmother for you. I kept
away from her. I had more sympathy with her during my
early twenties, though, when I had already left home.

As a child, I didn't like explaining why I have a peculiar
name. In the north of England, a foreign name is not that
common. 'Pardon?' they used to say. You know, I wasn't
very forward. I was a very shy child. I was so embarrassed
by having a foreign name because no one could pronounce
it. If you were a very forward kid maybe it wouldn't bother
you. People used to say, 'You've got a funny name.' I told
you that I had a long nose while other kids seemed to have

snub noses, and I had a brother who was mentally retarded and no one really understood what that meant, despite the fact that the sister of one of the girls at school had Down's Syndrome. All this made life very difficult.

My brother is two years older than me and mentally retarded enough to need, not constant care and attention, but a certain amount. He can't read or write very well. He also needs help in various things and can't make decisions for himself. He can go out to work and do a simple job, though. In some ways, now, he is like a six-year-old and in others more like fifteen. As a child, I was very jealous of him. He didn't get told off for a lot of things I got told off for and he used to get more attention than me. 'Why does Howard get away with these things and not me?' 'Because he's mentally handicapped.' 'I'm fed up with Howard.' You see, when Howard was very young he used to play with us and I didn't realize that there was anything wrong with him. There was something a bit odd, but I didn't know what. Then he just moved further and further away from us as we got older. There was talk, at one point, of him going to a special school in Bristol, which was very hard to get into, and, in fact, if he had gone, he would have been just down the road from where my husband was brought up. We would have moved there too. But Howard didn't go. My father didn't think it was a good idea. My parents argued a lot over it.

When I was very young, kids would come around to a party on my birthday. There would be a cake made by Sam, our confectioner at the bakery. We would run around eating jelly and all these disgusting things and play games like Postman's Knock and Pass the Parcel, which I loved. I loved getting presents. The kids would bring me presents, probably nasty cheap things, but I just enjoyed the whole thing. I wasn't that bothered or fussy. These days I am *very* fussy. My birthday is in the summer and I remember my father giving me a present of some popper beads one year – those plastic popper beads which were really popular. I really loved them. This one birthday – which must have been in 1955 or 1956 – he gave me a whole set of popper beads in different colours and I spent ages putting them together and pulling them apart. As my father worked nights, he would sometimes stay up in the early morning just to see me. I remember this one birth-day when we were living up above the bakery, him being there and giving me these popper beads.

I used to have kids over to play quite often and we were fairly unsupervised. 'Thou shalt' and 'Thou shalt not' didn't come into it much with my family. In some ways, my parents seemed terribly unconcerned. There were certain things they didn't like, such as me reading the *Beano* and the *Dandy*, but on the other hand they didn't get into a tizz about quite a lot of things. We used to play 'Black and White Rabbit', which is knocking on people's doors and running away. You hid round the corner and laughed when they answered the door. We used to do some terrible things. When I was about five, we let the tyres down on my father's van.

I went to Brownies for a while, but I was a terrible Brownie. I was shy and didn't like doing communal things like going to camp and sleeping in bunk beds, all those sociable and gregarious Brownie things. But I wanted to be part of it. I didn't want to be left out, so I started trying to join in. I even got as far as being Sixer, which is the head of a Brownie patrol. I forced myself into it. I always felt like an outsider, everybody thinking I was peculiar and odd. So I pushed myself into becoming a Sixer, though maybe I achieved that status because I'd stuck around long enough and got my badges. My parents didn't help me with Brownies. This wasn't because my parents couldn't be bothered, it was because it never dawned on them that they might have been helpful.

I used to sit in my room a lot and daydream. Blue was my favourite colour and my bedroom was blue. I didn't really read until I was nearly eight and the first book I can remember really was a Noddy book. As my parents didn't like me reading the *Dandy* and *Beano* – I suppose they really thought it was bad for my reading and bad for my education – I thought it was terribly naughty to have them. My husband's parents were fairly strict and conservative in many ways, yet they let him read these comics. I had to be really sneaky. I was allowed girls' comics, though. My favourites were *Bunty* and *Princess*, disgusting girls' comics, which I used to devour. I absolutely loved them.

When I was eight and we moved to the second shop, we had a little garden. Then Prince came. Prince was my dog. He was a Welsh border collie. He was a ruffian and I adore him to this day. I sometimes call my husband 'Prince' by mistake, but Richard knows that's a compliment! I really adored Prince. He was got specially to be my dog and I was supposed to look after him, but because I was still very young, most things were obviously done by my parents. When he was only a baby, he would walk along and do the splits in the middle of the kitchen floor. I would just laugh and my mother would pick him up and put him at his bowl. When he peed on the floor, I used to giggle. At eight, I was no good at looking after him. I wasn't any good at training him, either. I had to be taught to train him in the end, because he used to get very wild and excited. I was in my twenties when Prince died and he was sixteen. I was living away from home then. Prince and I grew up together really.

We went to Butlin's one summer, which as a kid was great. We had a chalet – my mother, my brother and I. My father had to stay at work, but he came down to visit one day. This was 1958 and it was a glorious week, absolutely fantastic sunny weather. I suppose Butlin's was tacky, and I had the vague feeling that some of the things we were doing, the organized games and competitions and the Red Coats were a bit embarrassing. There was all this stodgy English food, chips with everything. But for kids, it was a whole week of endless swimming, roundabouts and excitement. It was all there and cost nothing extra. My mother took us because she thought it was a good way to keep us entertained. To me it seemed the ultimate fairyland.

On Sundays, my family would often go to watch

cartoons at the local cinema and then go on to a Chinese restaurant in Manchester. My brother hated the food and always ordered egg and chips as there was English food on the menu, but I loved Chinese food. In fact, my favourite food, as a kid, was rice mixed with bits of things. I used to lie in bed at night thinking, I want some of my favourite food, rice and bits. As my parents didn't know much about Chinese food, they let me order what I wanted.

We saw all this Disney stuff at the cinema – I mean tons and tons of it. And when I was bigger, we would go and see feature films. I remember seeing *South Pacific* when it first came out and *The King and I.* This was the 'real' world, real life, to me. I planned to go out and find this wonderland. Why I was living with my parents in the way we were was just some unfortunate circumstance that we had to put up with for now! I was going to be stinking rich! I was going to go to Hollywood! I was going to be in the movies! As far as I was concerned, I was going to live like a princess. Anything that was going on around me, things like my cousins getting married, my parents worrying about whatever they were worrying about, people waiting to get houses and mortgages, these things would never happen to me. I just had this vision that I would get out, I would not live this way when I grew up. I was bloody determined I wasn't going to stay with what I knew. Life for most people around me in the Fifties seemed so dull.

# MARIANNE

My grandfather had emerged from the Thirties and the war years to own his own tanning business on the North Shore of Massachusetts. It was called Flynn and Whipple Company and he had had a partner, obviously Mr Whipple, as we were the Flynns. When Mr Whipple died, my grandfather bought out his widow so that the business became solely my grandfather's, though he kept the partnership name. Most factories did very well out of the War and Peabody was a town where the tanning industry really did boom. Grandpa Flynn had as many as twenty-five employees during his hey day and by the time I was born, in 1946, the whole family was doing very well. We lived such an affluent life for much of the Fifties, we must have earned an awful lot and spent it just as soon as the cheques cleared. There was plenty more where that came from!

Grandpa Flynn, my father's father, always bought Cadillacs, so we had the flashy trappings of success. Now as far as money in the bank was concerned, he did make a good few pennies, even in comparison to the blue-blooded Yankees who had been in New England for many generations. He made as much money as all but the very wealthy, and contributed heavily to churches and hospitals. Grandpa Flynn himself was never in politics in Peabody but he easily could have been. He tended to support candidates of his choosing and probably did have considerable influence and power over the decisions made in City Hall, even though he was not the person out front taking responsibility. He always gave money to elect the men who could further his interests.

The Flynn's didn't have Cadillacs right from the beginning but when my father was growing up, his family had cars whereas my mother's family didn't. I first remember we had Plymouths, which were moderate family cars, and then we moved up to Oldsmobiles.

Grandpa Flynn had the Oldsmobile 98 which was the top of the line and all his children – my father and my aunt and my uncle – had the Olds 88. They couldn't have such an expensive car as the 'Big Fellow', they had to have something slightly less grand. Then, when it got to Cadillacs, my grandfather would have the biggest, the longest, the best, and my father and my aunt and my uncle would get the next size down.

Grandpa Flynn bought houses for his daughter and his other son but we didn't get one because my mother was Italian. There was definite prejudice. The Santa Marias had a steady and stable income but they would always have been considered lower middle class in terms of their actual status in the community. The undercurrents and the seeds for my parents' later divorce were sown very early on, although as a young child none of this touched me. Life was wonderful. I would go out into the fields and my memories are of little blue flowers growing, just little spats of them here and there, and if I could find and pick those tiny blue forget-me-nots, I would be thrilled. I'd lie on my back and look at the clouds passing by, making pictures out of them.

My mother's parents were immigrants. My grandfather worked as a mason and during the Depression did a lot of ornate fireplace work on the mansions in Beverly Farms. He was very talented and a good artist. When he was out of work, he drew from memory very detailed, almost architectural, drawings from aqueducts in Italy and he played musical instruments, the tuba and the guitar and maybe a bit of the violin. There was a band at the Italian Club and Uncle Joe played the violin in it. Even on my father's side, my grandmother played piano and sang. Grandpa Flynn's brother owned a radio station in New Hampshire and had an orchestra. Once he played in a band with one of the Dorsey Brothers. And so in these families there was a musical heritage. It was never particularly professional, but was nonetheless a presence.

The Santa Marias never had much money. They had their garden during the Depression so that they were not starving like a lot of other people, and there was also a certain stability in that my grandfather had built his own house: they were not renting from anyone. Grandpa Flynn lived in Peabody and only went to school till twelve or thereabouts. He was kind of a rough tough little Irish kid and there were no jobs around except for at the Bleachery. What the Bleachery did I don't really know, but all the other factories had to do with skins or textiles.

My blue forget-me-not fields were behind where we lived in a two-family house with my Italian grandparents; they lived downstairs and we lived upstairs. There was a front door, and we tended to use that, but we also had a back door which led up some stairs to our 'house' and there was no entrance that way to my grandmother's. She had her own back door. We had a kitchen and bath upstairs and they had their own downstairs, so we were all self-contained. What is strange about this arrangement is that we lived in the country and all the other houses there were for single families.

I remember the house as being wood-shingled, painted white with brown trim, and it had a little front porch we later closed in. My grandfather built it when he came from Italy and my mother and her two brothers (and two other children who died when they were babies) were all born there. The house was built specifically for two families because relatives coming from Italy also shared the house. It was expected that you would provide your relatives with accommodation until they got their own places to live. In consequence, my neighbourhood was entirely family and we all lived in one road.

This house was in Danvers, a town next to Peabody, where the Flynn and Whipple factory stood. In general, the area was rural. There had been a lot of farms there when my father grew up and he had always done farming as a boy. But where I lived, the land was mainly fields and hills and woods and we lived at the top of a hill, with a main road at the bottom. When I was little, all the mail boxes were in a row at the bottom of the hill and to get your mail, you had to walk all the way down to the main road and climb back up again. It seemed a long way.

I lived on that one street from the time I was born until my parents separated when I was seventeen. In 1953, my parents decided to build our own house across the road. I was seven. From the very beginning, my experience of living in those two houses was very good. I think I was probably quite happy as a young child, living in that secure environment, being doted on by old Italian ladies. It wasn't a very American upbringing, in one sense, but my father added the Anglo-Irish influence, and so there was a cultural mixture right from the start. My cousins, two houses down, had more of a strictly Italian day-to-day lifestyle and yet they seem more American to me now. There must have been a lot of choices and you could pick up on as much or as little of the Italian as you wanted. I tended to pick up on most of it.

People spoke Italian around me all the time. When I was little, before I ever went to school, I didn't differentiate between what was Italian and what was American. It was all just what I knew. The bits of it that I remember best concern my grandmother and my grandmother's friends. They are happy memories for me. One particular friend of hers, who I liked very very much, didn't have any children so she really spoiled and petted me. Between the two of them, I was the spoiled little princess, but not in a material sense, with money and presents. They were very poor, they had nothing. I was over-indulged in a very simple, peasant way, with love. I can remember sitting in my grandmother's house and she would be crocheting and she'd have on some TV show, or be listening to prayers on the Italian radio station. There was a broadcast from Boston, where there was a lot of immigrant influence, but my grandmother did not want to live there. Her relatives, who were called Paysans and who came from the same three or four towns in Italy, all emigrated to America around the same time, and we had family living in Boston. My grandmother didn't like the city at all. Her family had come from the mountains and she wanted the countryside. She was a very determined person and, once she knew what she wanted, it just had to happen exactly as she said.

My grandfather always had a very big garden next to the house and he grew lettuces and onions in a wooden cold frame with a glass top, which was there to protect the lettuces and the more fragile vegetables. You would just lift up the glass to see how the plants were doing. There were rows and rows of tomato plants. We grew green beans, carrots, green peppers, parsley and mint, and my mother had a red rose bush right at the back door, which I always loved. She would always have a few rows of gladiolis growing at the very end of the garden. Sometimes we would have corn, and sometimes we wouldn't, as it wasn't an easy thing to grow. In the garage, there were always tomatoes on a stand left to ripen. My grandmother would can the tomatoes and she would make her own pasta and ravioli.

When I started school, the differences between the American way and the Italian way became more apparent and when my mother would make a sandwich, she would say, 'What kind of bread do you want? Do you want American bread?' Our usual bread wouldn't be called Italian bread. The Italian bread was 'The Bread' and the American bread was 'The Other Bread', so that the Italian influence predominated. To school I might bring a salami sandwich, which was an alien food in Peabody, with mostly Irish Catholic children. They would bring peanut butter and jelly sandwiches, or tuna, maybe peanut butter and marshmallow for a change, all on Wonder Bread. And those kids would always put butter on their sandwiches. We never put anything on ours. We just had the bread and the meat and the cheese, and the cheese was provolone cheese, never American processed cheese.

My mother would also make these nice hot lunches which I would feel guilty about. Sometimes she would put thick minestrone soup or a hot dog in my thermos so I would have a nourishing meal and I would be too embarrassed to eat any of it. I used to throw the food away or I would bring it home again. I was so mortified that I was not like everybody else. These were just tiny things, but looking back on it, there was such a cultural contrast between my home life and my school life. If I had gone to an ordinary state school, there would have been a wider variety of ethnic backgrounds to contend with and plain old American culture being promoted over everything. But my school was an Irish Catholic parochial school run by nuns. There were only a few Portuguese children and an Italian thrown in for balance. And due to the fact that my Irish grandfather always gave big bucks to this school, because this was his Parish, the Irish half of me got totally bolstered during the school day. Then I would go home to an Italian household. It led to a good case of schizophrenia later on!

My father was very attracted to the Italian culture because his family were brawling Irish. He probably found that people weren't any less strict but in telling you what you should do, the Italians practised it too. I remember the Irish would say, 'Oh, we never talk about this', but what they did might have been another story. The Italians really did practise what they preached. Both lifestyles had a strictness because they followed the Catholic religion and that was familiar enough not to seem strange to Daddy. What he liked was the apparent looseness of a sort of 'eat, drink and be merry' household. The Flynn's had an 'eat, drink, get drunk, get in a fight' lifestyle with a lot of guilt and remorse thrown in. The Italians believed in moderation and they were happy and loving and there was no undercurrent of feuding or ill-will. The real difference might have been that my mother's father was not by nature a violent man, although he was the head of his household and old-fashioned. I don't doubt he would have hesitated to give his children a good crack if they had talked back to him or disobeyed, but I don't think he would indiscriminately bully. Around Grandpa Flynn, you had to be careful what you said, and when you said it, and even if you did all the right things, there was no guarantee that for some bizarre reason (probably his drinking), he wouldn't just fly off the handle. He couldn't just be happy to *be*.

With all this Italian and Irish influence, I don't really know how I came to wear very English clothes, but they were cute. My mother must have liked tartans and they were a very popular line in the better-quality American children's clothes during the Fifties. In the photographs that I have, I focus in on the ones where I am wearing little plaid outfits. Ever since I was very little, I wanted Scottish kilts, anything that was plaid, or any Scottish music. I had to have these things. When we flew to Florida with my father's mother for a winter vacation in 1950 – I was three – I had a little two-piece bathing suit with a palm tree on the side made from cotton. It was red tartan with a ruffle on the bottom and we bought it in Palm Beach. I loved it because the style was cute and it was plaid. And I have a snap of my new-born brother with my father and me standing beside the baby carriage. Again I am wearing a little plaid. This one was mainly red, a smocked dress with a bow on the back with argyle ankle socks and either red shoes with straps or black patent Mary Janes. I just loved that dress and wore it all the time. Once my mother was going to send some clothes to relatives in Italy and I couldn't find a particular little red wool plaid pleated skirt that obviously she had boxed up to send to them. I went crazy at her because I didn't like any of my plaid things to be missing. And if I heard Scottish music or Irish music when I was small, it seemed to me as if there was a sort of yearning in me to get to some secret homeland I could never quite reach.

Maybe once or twice a year, at my birthday and Christmas, my mother and I would go to Pattee Anne. This was an exclusive children's clothing store and Grandpa Flynn would give me fifty dollars to buy clothes with. It was a lot then. We sometimes ordered clothes from the Best & Co catalogue, sent from Boston, and I remember these solid colours of red and navy and white in that catalogue and more conservative English-type clothes, more that traditional conventional style. I loved to look at the catalogues, particularly the one from F.A.O. Schwartz, the big toy shop in Boston which sold huge Steiff stuffed giraffes and lions as big as real animals. Of course, we never ordered anything like that.

I have a feeling I didn't go shopping very much as a little girl. My mother shopped and mostly left me home with my grandmother, but I do remember going down to the bottom of the hill and crossing the main road with my grandmother. We would then walk past some dirt roads to where chickens were kept, and we'd buy some chickens from a man and take them home in a burlap bag. The chickens would already be dead and we'd pluck the feathers in the back yard. I watched my grandfather plucking these feathers with horrified fascination. I don't think I dared to touch them but I could have if I'd wanted to.

When we needed goods a department store would sell, we went to Salem where they had two big stores, Almy's and Webber's. Salem was five miles away and was more like a city. It's famous for the old Puritan witch trials. They have a house there called The Witch House and I was always disappointed in this. You would expect to see witches and magic things but it was merely a very old house where the witches had been tried. I always felt let down. At Christmas, I remember going upstairs in Almy's, going to the upper floor, and they had a special section where the children would have their picture taken with Santa Claus. If you had a photo taken, which your parents would obviously have to pay for, you got to dip for a present in these bins covered with thin Christmas wrapping paper. I would get very excited to go and see Santa and get a cheap present, usually a colouring book or paper dolls. I took it for granted I was meeting the real Santa and not some man in a red suit doing a seasonal job.

We tended to go to church in neighbouring communities, Danvers or Beverly, and we sometimes went shopping in Beverly, taking my grandmother to the Italian grocery stores. We also used to shop in the regular grocery stores there, because my mother and father thought the quality of food was better. Later on, we had things delivered from S.S. Pierce, which was like Fortnum's or

Harrods. Now, this was my father's extravagantly epi-
curean desire for the good life. Buying from S.S. Pierce
generally meant paying twice as much as getting the same
thing from an ordinary grocery store. This is long before
supermarkets and malls flooded the area in the Sixties.
Much of that countryside is now megastores and parking
lots.

From what I have been saying, it seems that I lived a
very isolated childhood and was allowed to do much as I
wanted until I went to school. And once I got out of school,
as an adult, I really tried to regain the freedom of those
first five years of my life. I felt that here was the key to
who I really was and I should at least tap into it to see
what I wanted to make of myself. Of course, I quickly
eliminated twenty years of conditioning and went back to
being five again. You might say that was the late Sixties'
and early Seventies' influence as well. In any event, there
doesn't seem to have been anything horrible lurking in my
background upsetting me so much that I couldn't enjoy a
simple carefree life.

One of my aunts always felt that I had artistic talent.
She would say, 'Marianne was so sweet. She was three and
going to see Michael (her son) at his piano recital and most
children would be climbing all over the chairs but not
Marianne. Just give her a paper and pencil and she would
draw and be happy to sit still', and I think this was true. I
would go to my grandmother's house and she had a drawer
that had paper and pencils in it and I would get through
reams of paper, just drawing all kinds of things. As I got
towards my teens, I was always drawing dresses on girls
and fashion designing. I probably drew something every
day. When I appreciated nature, it was in the sense of
loving the pretty things, not the more earthy reality. There
was a particular tree in my grandmother's back yard
which I liked to sit under because a certain very soft grass
grew there which had a blue tint. It was a special magic
spot because the rest of the grass was ordinary green with
lots of clover. There were blackberry bushes right behind
the tree, right along the stone wall, and those things made

me happy. It didn't take much more than that for me to
be content, for me to just sit and think and dream. I don't
think I cared whether I played with the other kids or not.

Since our neighbourhood was so much family, there
were lots of cousins around. My cousins liked to play
indoors, and even though I did like to do the indoor things
of playing house and board games, I preferred the fields. I
used to try to make daisy chains but could never figure out
how to do them. They'd fall apart. I'd see daisy chains on
television or in pictures and I wanted them badly. I loved
wearing costumes and going out to dance in the street. We
put on shows in my big garage and it worked like a huge
echo chamber. I would sing and tap dance and be the star.

There were certain cousins I liked, such as my cousin
Kenny. He was about a year older than me and was fun to
play with. And sometimes Kenny's sister, Lois, would take
care of me. When I was older, in the late Fifties, she would
play Little Richard records on her portable record-player
and we would dance to the music. She was a teenager. I
didn't know anything about teenagers, I was really
oblivious to all that meant, but I liked to rock 'n' roll
about, probably with a lot more enthusiasm than style.

My mother liked sewing and she made sets of twin
dresses that we had the same. These Mother-and-
Daughter dresses were really quite the in-thing in the
Fifties. One set was really cute although Mom never quite
finished hers. The dresses were made of a cotton print in
light blue and beige. It was a funny sort of print, not a
floral – maybe geometric – and there was a white organdy
apron that buttoned on the front at the waist and at the
top, like the front of the apron. This had lace around the
edge and morning glories with leaves in blue and green
organdy appliquéd onto it. I still have the little apron that
went with mine somewhere. I wore it a lot. I was dressed
up as a matter of course and I always wore a bow in my
hair. My mother would buy me overalls, sometimes, and
attempt to send me out to play in them, but I didn't want
to. I always wanted fancy dresses and everything to
match. I think my grandmother encouraged me because

my mother had been a tomboy. Grandmama was glad to indulge herself when I came along and I was just happy for her to do it. So my poor mother was sort of left out in the cold. These days the situation is reversed: I buy my daughter all these nice little Benetton outfits, everything matching and outrageously expensive, and she wants to wear baggy old T-shirts and jeans and leave her hair unbrushed.

It seems I got left out in the cold the minute I went to school because I really was back a generation with my Italian childhood. I wasn't used to the rough and tumble of the streetwise Irish kids. But I didn't spend much time with the other children because the nuns wouldn't let you talk and at three o'clock, I was picked up and brought back home to my mother in the car. It was on Grandpa Flynn's direction I went to school in Peabody and it was pretty far to go. My father would drive me there on his way to work. The first nun who taught me was nice, but many of the others were terribly severe.

Before proper school, I went to a private kindergarten, closer to home, with probably a cross-section of kids there. You had to walk up many steps to a large porch and then up some more steps to a second floor where the kindergarten class was held in one large room. I remember walking upstairs one fine Fall day, just after Hallowe'en because we still had construction paper pumpkins and ghosts in the window, and seeing part of a dead deer on the porch. Obviously, the husband of the teacher had shot this deer and left the corpse on the porch. I never wanted to go back to kindergarten again. But hunting is a part of New England life and many fathers used to go off up Maine during the deer season to shoot 'Bambi'. Butchering a dead stag on a house porch would have been taken as par for the course, like plucking chicken feathers, and no one seemed squeamish about it except for me.

One story my mother told me and I think it is true – although I may have a tendency to embellish these things, to make them more dramatic, more sad or happy than they really were – is about how she once was going to a funeral. When I asked her questions about it, she explained that there had been a little girl who caught a cold and she lay down with her mother to take a nap. When her mother woke up, she found her little girl had died. This has stuck with me for thirty-five years. It made me sad, then, but it stuck with me because I worried it was going to happen to me. Maybe most kids don't take these things to heart, I don't know. I always had a sense of mortality although I didn't know specifically what was going on in the world and about people suffering. I remember very early on feeling this undercurrent of emotion for the whole human condition. It may have filtered through, unspoken, from those older Italian ladies I so liked to be with. They always dressed in black. There was something in their characters that I responded to; or, in what they had experienced in leaving their families at pretty young ages and coping with the hardships of being immigrants in America in the Depression. Other kids maybe didn't have a first-hand connection to this essential human sadness. They simply played all day and had fun in a really abandoned kind of way that I never could be part of. There was always this consciousness or conscience about everything with me.

I was taken to church from a very early age and I liked it. My father said that when I was a baby they took me to Boston visiting relatives. They had one of those baby books where people write things in about the baby. They wrote 'sang with the choir' about me. I enjoyed the music, the statues, the candles that you could light. As soon as I was able to, I lit the candles. We would always put money in this little box to pay for lighting a candle and, naturally, I wanted to light many candles. This is where I was spoiled. My father would give me enough money to light as many candles as I wanted. Most children probably lit one, if they were allowed any; and so I was indulged, but it was in the context of old-fashioned religion.

I remember when we got our television set so there probably was a time, for a few years, when we didn't have one. The TV was a huge, huge wooden box with a squarish screen that was flat on top and bottom and had curved sides. This screen was very tiny compared to the enormous box it was in. The picture tube was also enormous in the back. The set had all these tubes inside, too, so that when the TV repairman came to replace a tube he brought these long fluorescent light things. There was a machine in the Five and Dime where you could test your TV tubes to see if they worked or had gone dead.

Although my viewing was heavily monitored, occasionally I would catch a glimpse of something more interesting than cartoons or *The Lone Ranger.* I remember a little snatch of an adult programme and hearing the theme tune. That programme was called *Long Long Ago*, and it featured a rocking horse that was rocking without a rider. I don't know whether the rocking horse was empty because the little child had died or just grown up. Maybe it was even an adult mystery show or ghost story, but again the sadness of that opening scene really got to me.

One other bit I remember was also a scene from some longer programme, probably an adult play. A father had come home, and someone came to the door and shot the father. That always upset me and made me fearful that something would happen to my father! Early television was without the repetition of violence and weirdness that we have now. Kids today don't really pay that much attention to what is going on, because if they look away for two seconds something else is happening, and anyway, they know it's not real life. I think probably we were more impressed by what we saw because a lot of the programmes were live and very realistic and the sombre black-and-white picture added to its seriousness. In the Fifties, you didn't see or even hear about anybody who had been murdered, except on television, and so to view this scene without any explanation just really impressed me. Naturally once we watched more TV and got to see more violence, it became simply entertainment and had little effect on us. For the most part, we had to be in bed really early, so my brother and I watched mainly children's programmes. It could be that these two memories were the couple of moments when I caught a glimpse of something my mother never would have knowingly allowed me to see.

My favourite programme came on at noon on weekdays and I used to like to be off school sick so I could see it. This was *Big Brother Bob Emery*. Big Brother Bob played the ukelele to us 'Small Fry'. I knew who the president of the United States was, Dwight Eisenhower, because Big Brother Bob would propose a toast at some point in the programme and to a recording of 'Hail to the Chief', we would drink our milk in a toast while looking at the portrait of the President behind Big Brother Bob on the wall! You would hold your glass of milk and salute the President! In that sense, I realize I was probably immature in wishing to see these little kids' programmes longer than other kids, who were more clued in to *I Love Lucy* and *The Cisco Kid*. If I was at school and dreaming of Big Brother at noontime, that meant I was already in school until three in the afternoon and supposedly beyond the proper age for being a Small Fry!

I wanted to be on that show badly. It wasn't a question of not being allowed, it was a question of putting it together because it was local, live from Boston on Channel Four. My daughter, Grace, will say to me now, 'Can't I be on *Double Dare*?' And I'll say, 'Oh sure, we'll figure it out', and of course we never do because *Double Dare* is filmed in California and we'll never get there. People would just 'Yes' me to death and I'd forget about it for a while.

I also loved *Howdy Dowdy* and *The Mickey Mouse Club*. I know everybody switched over to *The Mickey Mouse Club* when it first came on in the mid-Fifties, and looking back on it, the shows were much more interesting. They had adventure serials like *Spin and Marty* and *Corky and Whiteshadow*. Whiteshadow was a dog and Corky was a girl played by Darlene, or one of the other Mouseketeers. All the kids at my school loved them, but the truth of it was, I was still loyal to Howdy Dowdy, who was rather silly and just a marionette puppet. But I liked Princess Summerfallwinterspring and her costume. She was an

Indian princess, and truly the fantasy obviously meant much more to me than this cowboy reality of a Walt Disney serial. Princesses and fairy tales were high in my book.

The Walt Disney and cartoon cult might have been at its height with *The Mickey Mouse Club*. The Mouseketeers were a bunch of moderately talented young teenagers who could sing and dance and act. And out in TV Land, we would put on our Mickey Mouse ears, watch these kids and wish we lived in California, too, so we could be Mouseketeers and go to Disneyland on our days off. There was a Mickey Mouse Club magazine you could buy and our parents very much encouraged everything Disney. It was safe, it was clean and it was good quality. The cartoons certainly were still made that painstakingly slow, old-fashioned way but since we were watching a black-and-white set much of the craftsmanship must have been lost on us.

I know we always had a telephone at home and the phone in the new house was in the kitchen. It was a red wall-phone – just the latest thing! At my grandmother's, we had our telephone in the upstairs hall and it was a black table model. You would pick up the receiver and the operator would say, 'Number please', and you would tell her the number you wanted. Our number was 1369M. My grandmother had a party line and she had a separate phone to us. Every once in a while we would get a little interference but I don't think we were on a party line, where you shared with other families. You did have to speak with the operator though. By the time we moved to the new house, Bell Telephone had modernized the exchanges and we had a dial phone. The numbers had changed too, to a prefix which was Spring 4, so we would dial SP4 and then the number. I used the phone quite a bit but they were all necessary phone calls, no chatting allowed.

The significance of any of the real American occasions was lost on me. On the Fourth of July, there would be a bonfire in Danvers but as we lived so far out of town, it seemed a great distance to go to this event where my parents knew people but we kids didn't. I didn't feel a part of all that communal patriotism. We used to go to a parade and fireworks in another town if that was considered a 'good' parade, but it was no big thing for us. You have to remember that these were small towns, no big floats or brass bands. We didn't do much to celebrate the patriotic way in school because the holidays conflicted with religious ones. In May, we would have to make the May Shrine while the public school kids would have a big do on Memorial Day. I was always hoping to be the one to take pink and light blue and white crêpe paper and decorate this orange crate. We would put a statue of Mary in it and surround it with crêpe paper and tissue flowers. I was dying to be the one who was chosen. Maybe because they felt I had artistic leanings, or maybe because my grandfather gave lots of money to the parish, I usually got picked. I showed no interest in anything else in school so when I did want to do something they probably encouraged me. The occasions which stand out in my life are religious, they are not the secular holidays. I certainly didn't like pledging allegiance to the flag. There came a point when I felt it was ridiculous and, as usual, I only wished to do the things that I really believed in. This was the beginning of the awareness which was to come in the Sixties: I didn't want to take what anybody said or follow anybody's rules and regulations without questioning and determining whether I felt these were right. So I fooled around with it in school. I moved my hand above my heart or below my heart and would mouth the words but not say them out loud. There was also a problem once I started developing a bust. You just didn't know where to put your hand without it looking as if you were giving yourself a little feel!

One national holiday everybody celebrated was Thanksgiving, on the last Thursday in November. Relatives would come down to us from New Hampshire and my aunt, uncle and cousin Michael would arrive from another part of Danvers. All of us – my brother, Skip, me, and my parents – would go to my grandparents' house. My grandmother would roast turkey but there was always an Italian dish as the mainstay. There would be just tons of Italian food. We kids would pretty much run riot and come and go as we pleased. Grandmama had a big rectangular maple dining table with matching chairs and there was a rocking chair and an old-fashioned stand-up radio in the dining room. The dining room was really the most used room in the house. The adults would sit around that table and drink wine and talk and eat and chat and yell at us kids and keep this going for hours and hours. The children would eat in the living room where my grandmother would set up straight-backed chairs with a tea towel over each one. We'd sit on footstools or ottomans and use the chair as a little individual table as there wouldn't be enough room for everybody at the dining-room table. The living room had big cabbage-rose wallpaper and was very drab. Then we'd watch TV and there would be a Shirley Temple film on or some Forties musical. We would tap dance and sing and grab whatever was handy to make costumes. We liked to play outside if it wasn't snowing. There were no restrictions on us except not to get in the way.

Once we moved into the new house, my mother decided that she would run a beauty shop from the garage and do hairdressing. It took a lot of organizing, but it eventually happened. She used to sell a product called 'Beauty Counsellor' which you couldn't buy in shops. You had to buy the range from a representative of the company. It was considered to be very good quality make-up so people wanted it. My mother set up three hairdryers and proper hairdresser's chairs. It was all very attractive. She picked out just what she wanted down to the special sinks. There was all this apparatus, permanent-wave rods and many kinds of shampoo and hairsprays and the garage got a nice linoleum tiled floor. In the little desk area, Mom kept the make-up and gifts and her appointment book. It appealed to me and I loved the gifts and hair ornaments she sold, hair combs with 'jewelled' tops and Revlon manicure sets, bottles of nail polish and cuticle remover. They were all packaged so nicely. At Christmas, all the products she ordered came in gift-wrapped boxes.

I used to go in and take what I pleased. As long as I didn't take too much I was allowed my fun and one way or another, I usually got my way. My mother used to try to cut my hair but she was scissors happy. She would love to snip away any time she could catch hold of me. There was a lot she would have liked to do but I wouldn't let her. Strangely enough, she would let me put a blonde streak in my hair with the bleach. I was allowed to do as I wanted with clothes and hair and make-up, things that I wouldn't allow my child to do! I had perms, I had haircuts, I had all sorts of new, fashionable hairstyles. She would get French hair magazines and I would go looking through them to find a hairstyle I thought was just so chic and, of course, at twelve, this is not going to look good. Nonetheless, we would try to do it. Once a real 'Twenties' look came into fashion and I let my mother do this extreme cut with my hair. It was not very successful.

Mom would have a tree for her customers at Christmas. It was metallic silver and she had a light wheel with three different colours: red, green and blue. You plugged it in and as the wheel turned, with the light behind it, the tree would change colour and be all shimmery and shiny. I felt it was beautiful and really outdid the real pine tree with ornaments we had in the living room. We always had angel hair all over our tree, gobs of it. I was never allowed to touch the tree as the angel hair was fibreglass and it would cut me. We didn't have a fireplace in our new house so my mother made a pretend chimney for Santa to slide down. In the back hallway, she put a big cardboard box wrapped with paper that looked like bricks. That is where Santa Claus brought the toys. We also had nice stockings made of felt which my mother had made herself. She wrote our names in gold lettering across the top. They were very simple stockings with yarn woven around the edges to keep them together and stuck on the stocking with glue was a white felt Christmas candle with a yellow flame at the top. It was the gold lettering at the top that I liked. When I lived at my grandmother's, we had fake plastic candles in the windows. They had small light bulbs for flames and we would switch them on at night so the people driving past could see them. Everyone did that and still does. There wasn't really a family Christmas tradition. I always wished that we would do exactly the same thing year in and year out with everybody taking part. I longed for the television image of the family around the piano, singing carols and drinking eggnog. But we didn't do any of this. It just went the way it went each year without any planning.

Most people on the North Shore during the Fifties didn't have much in the way of vacations because fathers only got around two weeks off for the whole year. What was common was for families to rent or own a summer house in the mountains of New Hampshire or Maine, and this would be used for weekends away. These cottages would be fairly primitive and could only be used in the summer because they would be snowed-in during the winter months. The roads to the lakes were never ploughed.

A family my father did business with owned some property in a place called Casco Bay, in Maine, and they had houses on a lake. In 1957, probably as a gesture of goodwill for their business dealings, these people let us go up and use one of the houses for a couple of weeks. It was a very rustic lakeside cottage but not one of the really creepy ones way in the pines with mooseheads on the wall. We went rowing in the boat and there were bloodsuckers and snapping turtles in the water. My brother would go wading into the lake and I might have, too, except they made this mention of bloodsuckers. Once I heard that, I would never go paddling. There are snaps of Skip in the lake throwing buckets of water to a little boy he had met there, and of me, on the stairs of this lakeside cabin, in a pretty dress with ankle socks and party shoes, evidently having nothing to do with this lakeside life except to lounge around and wonder what we were going to have nice to eat, if there was going to be TV or not.

Daddy must have got a local paper and I read that the local drive-in was showing Pat Boone in the movie, *Bernadine*. Well, didn't I have to go and see this! So one evening my family and I went and sat eating popcorn in the car at the drive-in. I came back singing that song 'Bernadine' over and over, looking in the newspapers for the enlarged photo they had of Pat Boone advertising this film. I would cut out the photo each time it appeared. This was my first crush on a movie star and I was madly in love, at ten, with Pat Boone, especially in that movie. I thought 'Bernadine' was just the greatest song and Pat Boone was so wonderful. I also loved the Everly Brothers and would dance around when they came on the radio. I liked Elvis Presley's 'Don't be Cruel' although I never cared for his more rocky hits, like 'Jailhouse Rock'. I didn't particularly like Elvis himself, preferring the more clean-cut Pat Boone type, the nice, romantic, teenage ballad-singer. The truth is I did not like that Fifties style of greased hair and souped-up cars and James Dean. My dreamboats always had the natural look and wore white buck shoes! Today, I can see how misguided I was!

# ELAINE

The way we were brought up, we weren't allowed to make a noise or fight outside in the street. We were made to come inside and the doors would be shut as soon as we started arguing, because the neighbours weren't to hear. I would not be able to cause a scene outside even now. We also never owed any money, although I remember a man used to knock at the door Wednesday lunchtime and if Mum didn't have the money on a couple of occasions, she would whisper, 'Oh, that's the so-and-so man, be quiet!' She used to have a Prudential voucher where she used to pay so much, a bit like a modern-day tally man. We would pay some small sum each week and then take our vouchers into certain shops like the Co-op. This would perhaps get us our school uniforms. We also had the Kleen-e-ze man come around with the cleaning materials he sold. He used to come to the door with a magic suitcase.

Our family lived in a house with a long back garden and a smallish front one. The back garden had an apple tree and a corrugated shed where Dad used to go. Our shoes never went to the cobblers to be mended because Dad used to buy bits of leather on the way home from work and he always did them himself. I think that was his escape, really, because he smoked and Mum disapproved. He could smoke as much as he liked down in the shed, and mend the shoes and be in peace. I can remember Mum saying, when she would nag him, 'Oh, what have you been doing down there? Smoking and snobbing!' Snobbing was mending shoes. All the shoes had leather soles, then. You got new shoes when Dad got his bonus and if your feet grew before his bonus arrived, you had to have the ends of your shoes cut out. Mum was very anti-smoking and really used to get annoyed. Dad used to smoke either Weights or Woodbines. And now three out of their four daughters smoke. When Mum did the housework, she used to wear a full pinny, one that came over the shoulders and crossed over and tied in the back. Dad used to wear blue drill bib-and-brace overalls to work with steel toe-capped shoes and a cap. Of course, he took his raincoat and a canvas shoulder-bag with his flask of tea and sandwiches for the day. The bag was khaki with brass poppers.

Our house was in the middle of a terrace with three bedrooms, a dining room, a sitting room and a very small kitchen. There was a large back garden and it was opposite some allotments. This was in Shoreham-by-Sea. The neighbourhood was pretty much working class but it was all private sector and we owned our own home. It was all residential and if you walked straight down the road, it was five to ten minutes' walk until you got to the sea. But you couldn't get to the beach directly from the house because there was a coal works and some light industry in the way. There wasn't any interference at all, though, from the works.

My younger sister, Janice, was born in 1951 and I wasn't aware of my mother's pregnancy. The style of the day was dresses on yokes or pleated and pregnancies were disguised. I only knew about Janice when she appeared. My mother had the baby at home and, being only five-and-a-half, I was sent away to Nan's, although my two older sisters were allowed to stay at home with Mum. It was always me who was packed off! I think, being the youngest, I was the most time-consuming and, as the third one down, I enjoyed having the bit of individual attention from Nan. She lived in Patcham in a flint-built cottage about ten miles away from us. To get there, it was a bus and a tram ride. First, we bussed into Brighton and caught a tram through the middle and we picked up another bus on the outskirts again. Patcham was just the other side of Brighton.

Nan didn't have electricity and there was only one gas lamp for lighting in her downstairs room. She just had that front room and a scullery, with an outside loo at the back and two upstairs bedrooms. She lived on her own. It was candles everywhere. Nan would save the ends of the candles and I used to model them into swans, animals and ballerinas. Once Mum had had Janice, Nan came over to help look after them both and I came back with Nan to this *fait accompli*. It was all very accepted, run-of-the-mill, when Janice arrived. There was no great fuss made about her because she was the fourth girl, anyhow.

It may be odd that I didn't know my mother was pregnant but she didn't know herself until she was four-and-a-half months gone! The story as Mum always tells it is that she wasn't feeling that well and my father discussed this with a workmate. He told this chap that his wife wasn't feeling right, feeling tired, and the workmate said, 'Well, my wife has been feeling the same sort of way and I have been buying her Iron Jelloids.' I think Dad bought her about three bottles of Iron Jelloids. They didn't make Mum feel any better so she went to the doctor. On her way back, she announced the news to Dad when he was working at the allotment. He said, 'Oh, well, never mind, well, that's it!' Dad was hopeful, still, for a son.

The allotment was big and Dad used to grow all our vegetables and soft fruit, raspberries and strawberries. I don't remember Mum ever buying much in the way of vegetables all the time I was growing up. He used to work on it evenings and weekends. His day job was working in Brighton at Allen West as a sheet-metal worker. When people used to say to me, 'What does your father do for a living?', I always replied that he was a *sheep*-metal worker. This was because we used to have farmyard animals to play with as toys and they were made of a lead-based metal. I honestly thought that he used to make the little sheep!

Dad was six foot, one inch tall, and very broad. He was a stern-looking man whose name was Frederick James but everybody called him Fred. He was very much a disciplinarian. There was always the threat, if you'd been naughty during the day, 'You wait until your father comes home!' We got good hidings and were sent to our rooms without tea. By about half past eight, although it seemed much later as a small child, Mum would come up with milk and biscuits but that was it. You were confined to your bedroom with no lights. They didn't know that I used to bring little bits of candle wax back from Nan's. Mum used to come in to me and ask, 'What's that funny smell?' I'd just say, 'Dunno.' I lit the candles because I was frightened of the dark.

We had electricity but Dad believed you shouldn't have more than one electric light on in the house anywhere you were. He would moan, 'Oh, the electricity bill!', so I felt I was doing him a favour, really, by lighting these candles. It was surprising I didn't set the bedroom on fire! I had the smallest room, the box room, six feet by five, and behind the bedhead there was a cupboard built into the wall in which my toys were kept. I stuffed the candles in there and would save them until the next time I was banished. There was just enough space for a bed and a dressing-table in my tiny room and there were cracks in the ceiling. All the wallpaper in the house was stripey and my favourite was a green and cream stripe.

The house was a couple of years old when Mum and Dad bought it. Mother was born in 1906 and married when she was twenty-eight, so the house was probably built around 1930. Although these were terrace houses, they were small terraces of fours, or threes or even twos. It wasn't one long building.

As a child, I wore a bonnet and a coat, a pair of leggings – rough and woolly and itchy – and ankle-strap shoes, which always posed a problem, because I have a very high instep and the strap would never go across my feet. I had to have a bit of elastic on my buttons so that they would meet. Usually the shoes were black patent, or in the summer, a white buckskin. The first hairstyle I really remember having was plaits. I had long hair, or rather I did until I cut one plait off in the first class of Infant School! I was about five and we used to wear knitted woolly bonnets which tied under the chin. One day I came home and Mum had a roaring fire in the grate. She said, 'Oh, take your hat and coat off and get warm.' She took my coat off but I wouldn't take my bonnet off. When I was eventually persuaded, Mum was horrified to see that one of my plaits was missing. We had had scissors and paper at school that day and I just got bored with cutting paper. I knew I had done wrong so said it was the girl who sat behind me. Mum went storming down to the school and after my disgrace, she said, 'It'll be short haircuts for you from now on!' and I had a parting and a slide. Dad used to cut it. He used to do all the really practical things. If you had a septic finger or a boil or needed a haircut, it was always Dad who did it.

We used to play out as a gang, because there was very little traffic, and you could run about in the street. We played tennis or put a skipping rope across the street and all the kids from the neighbouring houses would come. Where we were, the road was private and signposted 'Unadopted Road'. It was rough and you didn't get the through traffic. You didn't see that many cars, anyway, but no one much came down Eastern Avenue so we got very little traffic past our house. To the left was a little wood and a field where horses were kept.

Mum used to feed us up on a lot of boiled puddings. We ate very traditional food at home: dumplings and spotted dick, bacon rolls, and stews, particularly lamb stew. I didn't like lamb and still don't. Sometimes Mum bought a big tin of tomato soup and made dumplings to go in it and then grated cheese on top. I was given butter beans once and I didn't like them so they were served every meal for quite a while. I still wouldn't eat them. Once we went for Christmas lunch at Evelyn and Brian's just after they were married. Evelyn's my eldest sister. Well, I hated Brussels sprouts, but because they were taking a photograph of this Christmas lunch, I picked a sprout up and stuck it on my fork. When the photograph had been taken I took it off my fork again! My favourite food was Mum's treacle tart. But swede, even with carrots mashed into it, was revolting. It was always the rule that if you didn't eat it for this meal, you got it for the next.

I do remember rationing but only connected with clothes. We had knitted socks and knitted bathing costumes, which were all right as long as you stayed dry.

When you got wet and got the sand inside them, they were itchy. Mine was Fair Isle. They would hang badly around the bum. Nan used to knit the socks for us in a very coarse cotton and when your feet got hot at the end of the day, you could feel every stitch. They were so painful. We had navy knickers with elastic round and a pocket for your hankie. We also wore liberty bodices. I can remember Janice standing on the toilet seat and my trying to fasten the rubber buttons on her liberty bodice. They were very difficult for little fingers to manipulate. The elder one always helped the next one down to get dressed. As we got older and changed to stockings, we had liberty bodices with suspenders.

Mum had worked for a draper, The Scotch Wool Shop, before she got married. Her name was Lilian May Harcourt. She was a harassed mother but sometimes she would sing with us and she used to recite poetry. The poems were very long poems like 'Papa's Letter' and they always had a moral. But then, it was a very moralistic upbringing. She would recite to us when we would be sitting around the fire, after tea and before bedtime, or after school. We all liked the poetry. I think someone told me Mum's great grandmother was a poetess. These poems, though, would have been ones Mum had heard as a child and there were several which had incredibly long and involved stories. I can't remember any of them even though we heard them over and over again. And we would plead with her, 'Come on, Mum, tell us "The Mouse and the Cake"!'

We didn't have a car but we used to go on walks. Oh, I feel tired just thinking about it. We used to walk, all of us, Mum and the four girls in front and Dad following up behind. Mum used to chide him, 'Come on, you are always behind. You think you are a shepherd. You think this is your flock and you are a shepherd!' And we used to stop off at St Botolph's Church because Dad liked old buildings and museums. Even if we just passed it, we used to shout, 'Oh, there's St Botolph's!' We'd also go to the Pipe Museum which is still in Steyning and it is literally just a museum of pipes. These walks would start straight after Sunday lunch and there was a promise that when we got to the Pipe Museum, we could have an ice cream. I should think it was six miles. Ice lollies were just starting to come in and Mother used to insist that we had an ice cream because it was better for us as it had milk in it. Even if I wanted an ice lolly I couldn't have one – it was only coloured frozen water. I can remember Janice being carried sometimes so she couldn't have been very old. And once we had had our ice cream we used to walk all that way back home again.

We had our bath once a week. I can remember Mum talking, though, about Dad having daughters and that he wouldn't wash us after a certain age. We would be one after the other in the bath because heating and lighting were at a premium. It would be doubles, Dad doing one of us and Mum the other, a real assembly line! It was when I got to about eight that Dad didn't wash me any more. As soon as any of us started to approach puberty, he just stopped. For heating the water, we had an Ideal boiler which was quite old. It was in the kitchen and also served to dry the laundry as it had a line over the top. There were pipes running round from the boiler and the line was strung over the top of these. Mum did all the washing by hand. She has never had a washing-machine and boiled up in the boiler on top of the cooker. Later on, we bought an electric boiler but anything white was boiled separately. It was terribly hard work but she was meticulously clean. I had a feather mattress which had to be stripped and turned every week.

We all had chores delegated to us. My job was to red the steps and clean the brass door knocker. Our front door was oak. I also used to have to take off and polish everything on Mum's dressing-table. This dressing-table set was ebony and Janice has it now. Everything had to be cleaned and the dressing-table polished. This of course wasn't spray polish, it was all elbow grease.

In 1958, Mum and Dad bought a television for my sister Margaret's sixteenth birthday. I was twelve, then.

But we never did get a telephone or a fridge during the Fifties. The food was kept cold in a cupboard called a 'safe' and that had wire mesh over the front. A lot of people kept them outside the house, but Mum kept hers just inside the back door where it was cold, anyhow, because the kitchen floor was stone, redded, like the front door-step, once a week. The sink was an old butler, a deep earthenware sink with a wooden draining-board. Dad later put a metal plate over the top. When formica first came out, he cut some to fit and put a ledge round so the water didn't slop over the sides. Dad could turn his hand to most things and was quite a perfectionist in any job he did. He just did everything all jolly well. In the years after he died the house didn't have a lot of maintenance.

Our neighbours on one side were Minnie and Cyril Holloway, a brother and sister. He was a retired civil servant and they were really quite nice, quite genteel, more my idea of what I would have liked for grandparents rather than the ones I had. The other side were Mr and Mrs Clough who had a son and a daughter and he worked for the Port Authority as a harbour master. But we didn't speak to them. Or rather Mum never spoke to them. Just after Mum moved in, she was redding the top of her gate post and Mrs Clough came out saying, 'Are you trying to show me up, redding your gateposts?' And after that, those two women ignored each other for over thirty years. So we children could never speak to the Cloughs, either. But before Minnie and Cyril Holloway, there were the Spencers. They had a son, Geoffrey, who I played with quite a lot. We used to have snail races up and down the front garden path and when his snail won, I stamped on it! It was lovely. We would line up about a dozen snails and say, 'Right, those six are yours and these six are mine,' and we'd make the path wet in front of them so they would creep towards the moisture. It was a marble if yours won. You know, I'll give you my best marble, my one-er or my two-er. Marbles was the 'in' game. We also played jacks and hopscotch on the paving stones. When I was older and used to go to pubs, I'd try not to step on the cracks in those same paving stones to make sure I was sober when I got home. My parents never knew I went to pubs, they thought I was at a Youth Club. I was very young, under age, certainly, when I went to my first pub. We only drank cider and at the age of twelve, I could pass for sixteen. I was always forward.

For one glorious week, my parents rented a caravan called 'Blue Bird' in Bognor Regis. This was the year we had an extremely hot summer, probably 1959, and as with all hot summers, we also had the thunderstorms. Well, we had only been down there a couple of days when Janice and I had a scrap. During the course of this fight, I said to Janice, 'Oh, I hate you and wish you were dead!' So a little bit later on, when it began to thunder and lightning like nobody's business, Mother chimed in, 'There we are, the caravan is going to be struck by lightning. God heard you! You got your wish! Janice is going to be struck by lightning and she is going to die. That is what comes from saying wicked things!' And I howled! We were really excited, though, about this holiday. We had buckets and spades and also went to Bognor Zoo and saw the rabbit warren.

Usually for our holidays we would get sent to aunts. We had an aunt who lived in Watford, which was quite provincial, nothing like as urban as it is now. There were little shops and a little Co-op. It was very quiet and there were no cars. I went up by coach with Margaret and as we drove through Watford High Street, I remember seeing a black man and saying, 'Cor, look at him!' So everyone sort of looked then, and *they* all said, 'Look, a black man!' I can still see his face. That was the first time I had ever seen someone other than white. Our cousin in Watford, John, taught me Cat's Cradle but much more important, he also taught me how to get down to one peg in solitaire and I did love him. I thought he was wonderful because he was about my age and the only boy we knew in the family as we were all girls.

Very occasionally, we would go to our aunt in Tunbridge Wells and it was terribly posh. These were our rich relatives and Uncle George even had a car as he was a rep for Sharwoods. It was a black Austin A30. Auntie Olive was a very good cook and our cousin, Paula, was adopted. When we visited them, we would have to be on our very best behaviour and would get a lecture before we went in about saying 'Please' and 'Thank you' and minding our manners. Certainly, there were no elbows allowed on the table. If we did that, our father would hit our elbows with a spoon. As Paula was an only child whereas we were one of four, she was quite refined in comparison to us. Olive and George had a very nice home and a lovely garden, and so on, but you had to do everything to time there. They had to make sure before Paula went to school that she had had her bowels open and afterwards would ask her what it was like! I can remember Auntie Olive asking me that one day. I told her to mind her own business. Margaret has seen Paula recently but I don't know what I would say to her after so long.

Sundays were pretty full days, for besides our walks, we were trotted up to church twice a day. We'd change churches when Mum fell out with anybody and that was fairly frequently. And so, we went to the Methodists, then we went to the Baptists, and then the Congregationals, and we went to some Evangelists in Lancing after Dad met Mr Davis who was in the War with him. We didn't really have religion at home, though. Mum and Dad weren't ones for thumping the Bible, but Nan was, and every time I went over to Patcham I had to recite, parrot-fashion, the books of the Old and New Testaments. It was just a memory exercise. If I forgot two nights running, I wouldn't get any Horlicks tablets. They used to sell them in packets and that was my treat. If you were staying at Nan's on your holiday, you used to walk up this little lane through the churchyard to see Mrs Alfrey, Nan's sister. There was a memorial there with an angel. Just opposite, a line of cottages went down the hill and Mrs Alfrey had one of these. Her front door was always open. These cottages are probably worth a fortune nowadays. Because Mrs Alfrey had electricity, she had a radio, and we used to walk across and listen to *The Archers* at seven o'clock. There was a family of boys down the road I used to play with.

We all had wooden toilet seats and Nan's toilet seat in Patcham had woodworm. I was always afraid the worms would come out when I was sitting there. She didn't have a toilet in her cottage. It was in a shed up the back and two loos were shared between about four cottages. The toilet was very high. I remember going out Nan's back door and her kitchen used to always smell of OMO. She had a nice brick patio. There was a back yard but it was everyone's back yard and then there were these two little loos, one at either end. Unlike Nan, we did have a toilet upstairs in our house. We used to have Bronco toilet paper, which was waxed and hard, on a roll. It was crinkly and cream-coloured with *Bronco* written on the corner and if we ran out we had to use newspaper. I would have to cut it into six inch squares and thread these onto a piece of string.

When I stayed at Nan's, I never realized she had two bedrooms because I only ever went into one. We used to sleep in the bed with her and I would wake up quite early, longing to move my legs, but not daring to as I would wake her up. I was terrified that she would nag me for disturbing her. I used to inch my legs out and it could take me twenty minutes. There were always chamber pots under the bed. I would lie there dying for a pee and I couldn't get up! Nan was probably not as old as my childhood memory thinks of her, but women used to dress old. For years and years, she wore her hair in a bun and a felt hat with big hat pins in it. It was only a few years before she died that she had her hair cut off and Margaret permed it. She must have been very good, really, living out there with no electricity and no way of entertaining herself. We would sometimes play Snakes and Ladders, and cards. She kept things in play tins. She would make everything sound like an adventure, even going down to buy Blackie's fish off the fish stall. It all sounded wonderful but maybe it was just the change in routine.

Nan's name was Nancy Carter and she didn't marry my grandfather until my original grandmother had died. Because she didn't marry until she was nearly fifty, she didn't have any children of her own and then Grandad died and she was very much left on her own. I don't think Mum particularly liked her as she often used to moan about her. I remember Dad's father, Grandpa Chittenden. It was a terrible name to spell. I always vowed when I got married it would be to somebody with a simple name that everybody could understand. I married a Leigh and people still say to me, 'How do you spell it, Leigh or Lee?' Every time we said Chittenden, they'd say, 'How do you spell it?' Grandma Chittenden was quite tall and rather gaunt. She had these long curly grey hairs that used to grow out of her chin and I hated her kissing me goodbye because I didn't like the feel of them on my face.

I think that the Chittendens always lived in Shoreham but the family originally came from Kent. There were ships in bottles, two or three of them, at Grandpa Chittenden's house and stuffed fish in cases. I don't know where these nautical things came from but maybe from Grandma Chittenden's side because she was a Merrick and her father or grandfather was Captain Merrick, a smuggler. Captain Merrick's portrait hung in the Shoreham Museum. He hasn't been in there for a few years, now, but I used to always go and say hello to that oil portrait of him. I liked his red bushy beard. It is an old portrait and he has the seaman's cap, the big red beard and red hair. He had a lovely face. Mum used to always make a lot of that red hair.

Mum and Dad both had brown hair and Evelyn and Margaret do too, but I was born in 1945, at the end of the War, when Dad was away. When Mum suddenly produced this baby with very red hair, really carroty, a few tongues wagged! She was standing in the fish-shop queue one day and the lady behind her made some sort of remark, you know, about how it was strange that she had this baby with red hair when both parents had brown hair as did the other two children. Mum never spoke to her from that day on! All the way through, Mum made great friends with people and thought they were wonderful and would spend a lot of time with them. They might then put a foot wrong, or something would be said, and she would drop them absolutely. I can never remember her speaking to all of her three sisters at the same time. This has happened with Mum and her daughters as well. I think there have been times, sometimes years, when she would fall out with one of us.

Auntie Blanche usually came to us for Christmas day. She was Mum's eldest sister and unmarried. Later on, she lived in Watford with Auntie Phyllis but for quite a while Auntie Blanche lived in Brighton. She worked for Moore's, which was a big garage. Auntie Blanche was very well dressed. She always wore a white silk blouse and black high-heeled patent shoes and there came a time when she had to have all her teeth out and have dentures. Of course, in those days they didn't put dentures straight in so she had to walk around without any teeth at all. She tended to cover her gums with her lips when she spoke. When she answered the phone at work she would say, 'Herro, dis is Maws of Bitin shpeakin' and it became a family joke. We didn't have a telephone at home and would go down the road to the local call box. A few of the neighbours did have phones but we would never ask to make a call. It wasn't the done thing. These telephone boxes were the old A-button ones and it cost fourpence to make a call. You'd put your pennies in and when the person answered, you would press button A. If there was no reply or it was engaged, you pressed button B and got your money back. The call boxes were *always* working.

Auntie Blanche would give you two bob if you went to see her going off on the train. Of course, she had the money. She was nice as well. She came down once a month and used to stay for the weekend, even when Dad was alive. We would meet her in Brighton. She loved shopping and when we went into Marks & Sparks, Auntie Blanche always bought something. She'd never go just to look. Once in a while, she'd treat Mum. Sometimes she would meet us in Jimmy's in the Steine, which was a restaurant like an up-market British Home Stores before there were British Home Stores. They did fish and chips and it was lovely. I used to go in and think I was the cat's whiskers to have fish and chips and an ice cream. I don't know how much it cost but it was a real treat. Jimmy's is the only place I can remember we ever went out to eat. I think Mum and Dad would have liked to dine out but there just wasn't the money with four girls and Dad only on a manual worker's pay.

When our aunt and uncle from Tunbridge Wells drove down with Paula to visit, oh God! They used to arrive on a Sunday and we would get delegated our jobs. One time Auntie Olive arrived and she touched the pelmet rail. I guess she must have been looking for dust – she couldn't have done it for any other reason – and inevitably she got dust on her finger. After that, every time she was due to come, Mother used to make sure that those pelmet rails were clean. My job was to clean the upstairs sink and put out a guest towel. I used to wonder why they couldn't use the same one we used but I would have to hang a clean guest towel over the sink, specially, because they were coming. We also put out Castile soap for them as opposed to our everyday Sunlight, and Mum cooked special things, a roast and hot sweet, or an apple pie. Ten of us would be sitting down in a dining room about twelve foot square and a tiny kitchen, eight foot long by six.

Of course for this visit, we would wear our Sunday Best. This was usually a floral cotton dress that somebody had made since Mum didn't do dressmaking. One lady down the road used to sew and made loose covers for our three-piece suite. With these Sunday Best clothes, the minute you came in the house you took them off and changed. I still do this. We had to hang up our clothes straight away. And we had to fold everything because it would 'take no longer to fold your clothes than to throw them down in a heap'. I'm not that careful now, I just chuck mine anywhere. All the years of nagging had no long-term effect on me!

Opposite the house, after the allotments, there was a path through to the next road and along this path was a piggery. I used to call in on my way home from school to

look at the pigs and piglets. Once they had a litter of
kittens and I begged Mum for this one particular kitten I
had fallen in love with. She eventually said, 'Yes, all right.'
I brought Sooty home in an enamelled bread bin, a white
one with blue writing on it. I staggered because it was quite
a long road and I couldn't have been much more than
about six or seven, I suppose. Eventually I was standing in
the back door with this bread bin and said, 'Mum, oh
you've gotta look at him, Mum, he has lovely blue eyes!' I
took the lid off and of course he was a farm cat and he was
swoosh out of this bin and straight under the boiler. We
didn't see him for about three or four days. Sooty was
black with a white bib and when I went into hospital,
Mum came up visiting one day and said, 'I've given your
cat away to Mrs Davis. I didn't want him anymore, he was
a bit of a nuisance, another mouth to feed after all.' I never
really forgave her for that. I was in hospital when I was ten
for osteomyelitis and septicaemia. I was very poorly and
thought I was going to die and to top it all they gave away
my cat!

We used to keep tortoises as well. They kept running
away even though we drilled a hole in their shells and tied
a bit of string onto it. Mostly it was Evelyn who looked
after the animals because she was the one who used to
bring them home all the time. We had three ducks, and
chickens for the eggs, so we would go up along the top road
to a farmer to get the fertile eggs if we had a broody hen.
One day when we got there, he had got some day-old
ducklings and we were very taken with these. So we came
all the way back on the bus again just to ask if we could
buy them because we wouldn't have dared to get ducklings
without permission. Mother said, 'Oh yes, duck eggs would
make quite a nice change from chicken eggs.' So we went
all the way back again and got these three ducklings. We
called them Widdle, Waddle and Wuddle and they all
turned out to be drakes so we never got any duck eggs
at all. I remember Dad trying to kill a chicken for
Christmas or Easter. He tried to wring its neck and it
was flapping around the garden. There's a knack to it.

You have to push the top vertebrae out, and he couldn't do it.

For our weekly treat, there was the Shoreham Ritz and all us children would go to the Saturday matinée. You used to get things like *Hopalong Cassidy*. Really, it was just an event to go along and look at this huge television screen, we didn't have any favourite film stars. And The Ritz was grotty despite its name. Shoreham was still very much a small town in comparison with Brighton or Worthing, which we considered a trip out. We could walk to the Ritz in fifteen minutes and sit in the dark all afternoon. It cost one and six and that was affordable. When *South Pacific* came out, it was the first picture with the wide screen and we must have seen it ten times as a family in Brighton. We bought the record, and *Oklahoma* too, but we weren't allowed to play *South Pacific* on a Sunday because it had the song *Bloody Mary* in it! Dad used to quite like his music and we had an electric gramophone. He had originals of things like *The Laughing Policeman* and *The Cornish Dance*. Earlier, though, we had a wind-up gramophone. I remember cutting out the cartoon characters and sticking them around the steel rim, winding it up, and watching the characters go around. That was kept in the front room. Most times the front room door was shut so we lived in the tiny kitchen and dining room. The table was pushed against the wall and only pulled out for mealtimes. It had three leaves. And there was a coal fire. Dad would chop the wood and fetch the coal quite often because we had an all-night burner in the dining room.

In the middle of winter, our bedrooms were freezing as there was no heating upstairs. The only time I can remember it otherwise was if one of us was ill and then Mum would light a fire in the grate. When Dad had just come back from the war, he did chimney-sweeping and window-cleaning, and he kept his chimney-sweep brushes and would do the chimneys out at weekends. He had been in the Medical Corps during the war and served in France, Belgium and North Africa. As he was in Belgium for quite a while, he set up a friendship with the family where he was billeted. My second name is Jacqueline, after their daughter. I think it was his way of saying thank you because he was living with them when the news came through that I had arrived.

My birth was quite traumatic. The family doctor we had had for years and years, Dr Partridge, told Mum that she was expecting twins and ought to go into a nursing home, so she booked into this private nursing home. It was mega-expensive but the Army paid half. When she went in on the date she thought I was due, the staff gave her castor oil and hot baths, and castor oil and more hot baths until she was fed up. So she said, 'I'm taking myself off home. I'll be back in a fortnight.' I think she must have already been in labour by the time she returned because I was born that same night. This nursing home wasn't just a maternity home. They had war-wounded and what have you and they were obviously quite busy. So they made up their minds that because they had had so many busy nights, no one was going to produce *that* night. The staff would get one good night's sleep at least. And they tied up the bell. In fact, I was born by myself because Mum couldn't reach the bell anyway. It was only when they came to do turns at two in the morning that they saw I had arrived. This was care in a private nursing home. Mum went into shock after that.

The recent War was very much a part of our daily life in the Fifties. If we walked under the footbridge to go to the beach, we passed quite a wide expanse of old foundations for presumably what had been houses or warehouses. It was derelict like that for years and years. These buildings had been bombed during the War and the site was all very overgrown with weeds. Dad used to talk about the War in the context of how it affected what they had to go without, but you would never get Dad to talk about things he had seen, the killing. The War was presented constantly as one of the reasons why we weren't allowed to waste anything. If I left my dinner I'd be told, 'You can't waste this because we have had to do without.'

When we were in the Junior and Primary schools, we generally used to come home for lunch. It didn't give you much time because by the time you got home you could only bolt your dinner and start off back again. The walk took twenty minutes. Once we got to the Seniors, my sisters and I had bikes. We'd go through phases of having school dinners as Mum always seemed to have a part-time job and if her job overlapped the lunch hour, then we would stay on for the school lunch. Mum's jobs were mostly cleaning although once she had a job in the kiosk at the front of Shoreham Station.

By the time I was ten in 1955, I used to have two and sixpence pocket money. I spent it on sweets and caps for our toy guns. When there was a gang of us, we used to play in the fields at the top of the road or on the opposite side where there were woods and fields and we'd have gun fights. My favourite sweets were Everlasting Sticks which cost a penny. I've looked for years and years to find them but they don't seem to be about any more. They were long, thin strips of a sort of toffee and you could chew them and suck them and lick and they did seem to last for ever. A slab of palm toffee, four inches by two, was threepence and it was also lovely. I liked the banana split flavour better than the strawberry or all-toffee. When I was at the Seniors and cycling to school, a threepenny bar would last me all the way there and all the way back as I used to eat half each way. I used to stick the other half in my saddle-bag for the trip home.

When I went into the Senior School in 1956/57, they were very strict on how we wore our school uniforms. You just *had* to wear your beret. All our accessories were emerald green – beret, jumper, tie – worn with a navy skirt and a white blouse. This was an all-girls school and initially we only had women teachers and a headmistress. I hated school, especially French. Well, it wasn't actually French I hated, it was the French teacher who had a down on me. It didn't matter how hard I tried, I could never seem to get it right.

I used to pal around with my little gang and mess about.

Once I played truant and I got caught. There was a girl up the road, Marie Philpot, and she was a real goody-goody. She probably didn't get the opportunity to be anything else but hadn't got the courage, either, although she was quite sharp academically. One of my best friends and I decided that we were going to take the afternoon off so we skipped out at lunchtime. Jean's parents owned a pub and her boyfriend, who was working, had the day off. We experimented with make-up and our hair and generally lazed around doing nothing, feeling slightly dangerous. But by the time I got home, the school had already sent a note asking me to please explain my absence. And it was little goody-goody Marie Philpot who brought it! I didn't speak to her again. I suppose I took after Mum in the sense that I could certainly hold a grudge!

I didn't really want to stay on at school but I wanted to be a nurse and you had to have your parents' permission to start the training at eighteen. Mum and Dad said that if I stayed and took my GCEs, they would sign the necessary forms for me. And so, after I had taken my mock exams, I got the nursing application and brought it home. My parents refused to sign it, because on one of the open evenings my English teacher had told them I was really good at English and she thought I would do well as a teacher. This fitted in fine with Mum's social snobbery. She got it into her head that I was going to be a teacher and when I presented her with the application form for nursing, she turned on me saying, 'No daughter of mine is going to empty bedpans for a living.' I was heartbroken. I said, 'Right, you have broken your half of the bargain so I am not keeping mine', and I walked out of school six weeks before I should have sat my GCEs. It was years later, 1971, before I got to do my nursing training.

Besides teaching and nursing, girls could do the short-hand-typing course which I wouldn't have minded. The options were two GCEs and shorthand-typing or six GCEs and I wanted to do the two GCEs, mainly because I felt there were only two subjects that I had a chance of getting a GCE in anyhow, English and Art. The school put me down for six, though, and I knew I didn't have a hope in hell of getting them all. Girls were just really beginning to open up in office work and if you had a flair for languages, there were some real career opportunities. Things were beginning to happen for girls, but only just. The worst fate was considered to be factory work, which is just what my mother told me I would end up doing when I quit school, mixing with the riff-raff on an assembly line. She told me to march myself down to the employment office. I surprised her by starting work the next day as a nurse to a dental surgeon in Southwick where I stayed until I got married at eighteen. The pay was four guineas a week and I got to wear a white uniform. I gave Mum the four pounds for my board and lodging, only keeping the four shillings for myself. She'd never admit that I had surprised her by doing well. I suppose it was a relief to my parents to get the extra money but they'd never admit it. At any rate, it was the closest I could get to proper nursing and I did enjoy it.

My parents' attitude to nursing really surprised me as my father actively encouraged me to join the St John's Ambulance because I had this medical interest and so had he. He thought the experience would always be useful. I don't think St John's has changed very much over the years – you learned bandaging and home nursing – and I got my certificates. I didn't go for the social life and I didn't care who else turned up, it was purely my interest and I went every week between the ages of eight and fourteen. When we'd come out, we'd get three-pennyworth of chips or a bag of Smith's Crisps. In those days, the crisps weren't ready-salted and you could salt them or not as the salt used to come in a little screw of blue paper. The salt was always down at the bottom which ever end you opened the bag. Mum gave me the money to buy a snack and I usually bought chips because they were delicious. The woman serving in the chip shop was a real po-faced old cow. I think she disliked children and if you get a gang of twenty suddenly appearing in your orderly fish and chip shop, all just wanting chips, you might be put out. She never smiled or anything. Mum used to get the family fish and chips sometimes from a different shop but it wasn't often. It was a treat because, with six of us, it worked out quite expensive, although fish was much cheaper than meat. She would also occasionally coat fish in bread-crumbs and shallow-fry it but she didn't like to do this. I guess she felt cooking fish was too smelly.

Although we didn't take much notice of events in the outside world or even in England, all of us kids became excited at the idea of the Coronation. This may have been because our neighbourhood was planning a street party, and come the big day, the street was closed off at each end and a long table erected down the middle. I don't know quite how this happened, but the day was marred by my fighting with Bobby, the son of a local Polish family. It was all over who won the War and how. I can remember saying, 'Well, we won, see!' I was never very good on politics and I had somehow got it into my head that the Poles were on the side of the Germans so I felt they had no right to be at our street party now. I lobbed a jelly at him. I hit him, too, on the shoulder. The party started mid-afternoon on Coronation day. In the morning, we watched everything on television at a neighbour's house. I can remember the Coronation coach vividly and thinking it was just like a fairy-tale coach. I really did believe it was made of solid gold. There were quite a few children in our street as families tended to be bigger than they are now and every family in the street turned out. An average family would consist of four children. There might have been as many as a hundred people celebrating in all and the children's party lasted until dusk. Once we had finished eating, the grown-ups tried to set games but it all drifted away from organization and we kids were just allowed to run riot. The party food was sandwiches and sweets, with orange squash and cherryade to drink. I think the adults may have had their own party later on.

The cherryade would have come from the Corona man who used to deliver soft drinks in a van to your door. You could get limeade, cherryade, Coca Cola, fizzy orange or ginger beer. We were allowed to have a choice of the flavour we wanted and mine was always cherryade. Everybody had the Corona man once a week. We also drank home-made ginger beer, made from ginger, yeast, sugar and water. Mum would brew this spasmodically. She'd start it off in a jam jar, and at the end of a week or a fortnight it would be diluted with water. We'd bottle it in brown cider bottles with rubber screw tops. If you were ill, tucked up in bed with a cold, Mum would make lemonade because she thought the lemons were good for you. She would bring a jug up and put it by your bed. There was never any ice, though.

Dad used to buy *News Chronicle* on the way to work and read it on the train. This was a national paper, a big paper like *The Times*, and cost a penny. He also bought the *Mirror* and on Sundays would buy the *People*, which Mum used to really hate because it had pictures of scantily clad women in it. Dad's journey to work first involved a twenty-minute walk from our house to the station and then he would catch a train from Shoreham to Brighton. He would walk the length of Trafalgar Street, which was quite a long street, and then catch a bus to Allen West on the other side of Brighton. He did that every working day for nearly twenty years, leaving at six a.m. and returning home at six p.m. It would only take him about an hour to get to work because the service was good. We'd go on the train to Brighton sometimes and it was dirty. There were first- and third-class carriages and 'Ladies Only' ones, which we would sit in if they were available. One of our treats in the school holidays was to go to Steyning Market and we used to catch what we commonly called the Steyning Stinker because it was steamy, dirty and smelly. The trip took half an hour, and when we got to Steyning, the train had to fill up with water. This was a red steam train. At Steyning Station, you would come in just alongside the market, where the cattle trains used to pull in to go straight into the market place. This was an animal market for the most part, except for a few boring bits of agricultural machinery.

# JACINTA

My mother considers her photos of me when I was little as treasured possessions because she likes to compare them with the second family she had at her change of life. I had just started having a family myself and, when I had my first, within a year she had her fourth child. There was another one quickly after that, so I have two much younger sisters. Mum thought that she had finished with family life and she got, well, a surprise isn't the word, she was frantic! She didn't know what to do. She and my dad had decided that they were going home for good because my dad didn't like England, although my mum adored living in London. Dad decided he didn't like the cold, didn't want to stay here any more and he was just going home to Barbados. So the pregnancy delayed them for another year. I was surprised by the new baby but not really shocked to that extent. At the time I remember thinking, How can she treat me like this having one at *her* age? I thought she was really old because I was sixteen. Now, looking at it, she wasn't old, but to me she had been there for ever. I couldn't believe it.

My original family was my father, my mother, myself, my sister and my brother. I was the first and my brother was the last. He is the only boy in the family and Mum adored boys. Anybody's boy is Mum's boy, you know, and she ended up with four girls. And I like girls and have ended up with boys. I now have four boys and one girl so it has turned out to be a reversed situation.

My parents had been in England a good four years before they sent for me. Because I was the eldest, I was the first to come and then the others followed later. It was winter when I came to England in 1954. I came by ship, the SS *Sorriento*, and it was a great ship to sail in but I'll never forget that journey. First of all, there was no one to come with me. I had to rely on someone who was travelling on the same ship to be like a guardian, and they got this

87

young lady to look after me on the journey over. When we got at sea, she was fine but I wasn't well at all. I was sick from the time the ship left the harbour. It was awful – I never stopped being sick. I had a lot of English money because Mum didn't want me to ask anyone for anything and she sent over all these warm clothes for me so I came with woollen clothes. It seems silly to send those clothes to Barbados with its hot climate but at the time I didn't think about that. Quite a lot of the journey was warm and so was the ship. Apart from the sickness, I couldn't stand the smell of the food being cooked. There was always this strong smell of curry and I couldn't take it. They had machines on the ship that would give you Cokes when you put money in and that was what I lived on for most of the journey.

So when we stopped over in Tenerife, I went out with this English money, and not having travelled before, I didn't know what it was worth. I took ten pounds and got a hand of bananas. I hadn't eaten for so long I thought this hand of bananas was a feast and I started to devour them. As a result, I didn't see anything of Tenerife because all I was interested in was eating something that would stay down. So I ate nearly all of them and what I didn't eat I took back to the ship with me. I had a cabin to myself, and because the young lady was sharing with four other people, she decided that she would stay with me in my cabin. She was a lot older than I was and there were chaps on the boat. Eventually, she just dumped me and not only did she dump me but she took all my clothes with her as well. When we docked, I didn't have any of the clothes I set off with. I was nine years old and had just been abandoned.

There was all this snow on the journey to London, everything was white. I am not sure where we landed but we took a long journey by train and all the luggage had to be loaded. It was my first time on a train. I couldn't really see anything because it was night and what looked like mountains, I now realize, was just hillside and countryside all covered in snow. It looked very very pretty. You couldn't see anyone outside, any people. We were just on this train and travelling, not knowing where we were or where the train was stopping. All the ladies from the ship sat together on the train. They were very caring in that they realized I couldn't eat. Then we arrived at the station in London and my parents met me and took me home.

My parents had bought a house because, typical West Indian parents, if they were going to send for the children they needed somewhere to put them. The house was in Mortimer Road, London NW10 (Kensal Green) and even now if I pass I always make a point of going down and looking at it. It is a terraced house in a very nice street which was quiet at the time. It seemed enormous. London seemed strange and different because there was no sunshine and it was so cold. It was bitterly cold. And Mum decided I needed to be bathed. In bathing me, she picked me all over like a mother hen to look and see what I had and hadn't developed. She was going for a thorough examination during this bath. I think I passed inspection! And then she got me into warm clothes. The strangest thing I have never got over is the way you had to have a bath here. In the West Indies, if you were well-off you bathed inside, if you weren't, you bathed outside. Either way, it was by a stand pipe. Where it was developed enough, you would have a proper bath and proper shower and everything. But England was different. We had to put this galvanized thing down in front of the fire and then fill it up with all these buckets of water which had to be heated on the cooker. For warmth, you had either coal fires or paraffin heaters and my parents had two paraffin heaters. I didn't realize what they were until I touched one and got burned. It was all so strange. I was bathed in front of this fire, which was really nice, and dried off, and then had all this big food. After all that journey and travelling, I wanted to eat the food but still I was very tired so I slept while I was trying to eat, and Mum was asking questions, and I was chewing and sleeping at the same time and trying to answer. I don't think I brought anything over from the West Indies for my parents. I was going to my mum, so that at the time was the important thing. I was going to England, I was going to leave all my friends and go to my mum.

In the West Indies, most people know about England. I think you are more or less taught the same way and Barbados is classed as Little England, so you know that while Barbados is a little country, it is more or less the same. What I was not prepared for was the way the houses were built. In Barbados, there were brick houses but they were bungalows, all on one level. So I was really taken aback seeing buildings that appeared very tall and houses that had an upstairs and downstairs.

Mum used to work at Selfridges. Now, everyone is going mad on designer clothes but then *all* my clothes were designer clothes. The only problem was I didn't know it and didn't pin any importance to it. None of the other children did either. In those days all the warm clothes – sweaters and that – used to be heavily embroidered with beads. I had all these beautiful embroidered things, dresses that were really nice. I would see all these 'Names' but wouldn't put any significance to them. Now, I would love to have them. I even had French knickers and lace slips and all-in-ones, camisoles. All these things I had and thought they were so revolting. I couldn't stand them, I wanted proper underwear and I thought I would die if anybody would see me in these things. Of course they were really nice. My mother had sent me bras in the West Indies thinking I had a bust but I never wore a bra until after my first child. I had nothing to put in one.

Mum liked her job in Selfridges and she was there for many years after I came. But she did two jobs. She worked in Selfridges during the day and in the evenings she used to get the train, pop home for what seemed to me about fifteen minutes but it must have been a lot longer, and start another job in the evening six till ten at Kodak. She used to walk to Kensal Green station and get a train there. My dad actually worked as a signalman on the railway. He used to work Queens Park, Kensal Green and Kensal Rise stations. Many days he just did with a packed lunch. On his way from Kensal Rise to Kensal Green station, he would stop indoors, pick up a flask with his dinner and take it with him and start a different shift so he was doing two jobs at the time. And that was the saddest part of my ever coming to England. My parents just worked all the time.

On Sundays, my mum was fanatical about cleaning. Because I was the only one, they had tenants in the house. In those days everybody wanted somewhere to live and everybody had tenants. I remember there was an English lady living downstairs with her daughter and husband. Upstairs, there was a back room with someone living in it. There was a room next to that with someone living in it, then a toilet. Mum and Dad had the two main rooms, so there would have been four rooms and a toilet upstairs. Then there was the bathroom. Only cold water came out of the taps, not hot and cold, hence the iron bath and water being heated up to put in it. When I arrived, I ended up having a bed made up for me at night in the sitting room which was the front room. The room next to it was Mum and Dad's bedroom. The first time I got a room of my own was when I started to work. It was only then I had my very own room. And I had to pay for it!

We liked the lodgers, they were nice. They were two men from the West Indies and then one moved out and a lady came in. Over the years we saw many people come and go. When the English lady downstairs eventually moved, my parents took over that whole flat so I had a room and my parents had the two front rooms which had a dividing door in the middle. You would push that door into their bedroom. That door was mostly kept shut so we had the sitting room, their bedroom and bathroom downstairs. There was also a back room and a kitchen. I would go out the side door where I could see all the trains and time them. I became very good at train spotting because there was nothing else to do. It was very very lonely for me. I remember I became very sad. I didn't like the idea that I was brought from home in Barbados and left so much on my own. Once I started going to school, I was told to be home after school so that I wouldn't get into any trouble. But home was lonely. Everyone was out. Many evenings, I know, I didn't always go home but, being the strict parents that my parents were, it was a hiding if I got caught. I remember about that time black and white televisions came in and I was asking for this telly. They talked as if it was so trivial to waste money on a black and white telly. Up to today, this very day, my parents hardly watch television. My dad does not watch television, period, and still thinks they are a waste of money. My mum now looks forward to serials. I have gone back to Barbados many times now and two years ago, the last time I was there, *A Woman of Substance* was on and that was something she tuned in every week to see. She would make sure she was home on time to see this serial. But they never got a television until after the time I moved out. Before I got married, the only thing I wanted to know before I would say, 'Yes, I will marry you' was 'Will we have a television?' It seems petty but it really sticks out.

My London school days were very negative. Because of the time of the year I came, I went into Chamberlayne Wood School. There are two parts to that school, one just at the corner of Mortimer Road – Harvest Road I think it was called – and I started off there and went on to the higher school, which is just up the road, for eleven-year-olds. I thought going to school was just to learn about things, but I had come from the West Indies where teaching was vastly different. My first impression was the way that people looked at me because even then I was made to feel different or as if there was something wrong with me. There was only one other black child in the whole school. Only one. I was the second. That was bad, it was tough. It happened that we were both in the same class and that made it even more difficult. The girl that was there before me was friends with all the other girls. She was part of it. And I was the outsider. To be starting a new school and to be black, it was something. Up until the day I left I don't think that I enjoyed being in my school. We were a mixed school, girls and boys. And the boys were the worst. The girls, even if they wanted to be friendly, stuck with who they knew. And the boys more or less picked on me. I understood from the West Indies that if I was in a class and somebody hit me, I should just belt the life out of them. That was me and I was a rebel and more or less a tomboy. So, when I came to school here and people started hitting me and picking on me for no reason, I wasn't going to take it. I just used to turn around and start a fight. I was then classed as disruptive and not settling down. Today I can look back on this and say very positively that the two teachers I had did not change in their attitude to me at all until the time I left school: I disliked them and they disliked me. Now I realize that they were prejudiced but at the time I did not know what was wrong. I just knew that something was not right. In the Fifties, I could never go up and say 'this person is prejudiced' or anything like that. These two teachers were husband and wife, teaching at the same school. I used to have the husband for some of my subjects but the wife was mainly my teacher. Whichever class I went in, there was always a problem. I remember at one stage, and if I think back carefully now I can remember as clearly as if it were today, that even from my time in the West Indies I disliked sewing. Today I don't do any sewing. I cannot stand it and she insisted, the wife, that I went into the sewing class. I would have preferred the cookery class. Now, cooking is something that I love and am always doing. I am prepared to save now to throw parties so I can cook and have people round to nice meals. And I wanted so much to do cooking but that teacher insisted I went into this sewing class. One of the things that happens to me, a trait or whatever you want to call it, is that I sweat very badly on my hands and my feet. So to hold material and actually sew, the fabric was always wet, it was always dirty. She reckoned I was doing it deliberately. I tried to explain but I was sent out of the class for not sewing properly. I had a terrible time. If the boys in class bullied me and I retaliated, I was the one who was sent out. So I had it from both ends.

I didn't discuss this with my parents because I think I would have got the blame. They believed that children needed a good hiding if they didn't learn and there was no harm in corrective punishment in school where my parents were concerned. I don't think that going home to them and complaining would have made much difference so I tried to fight my own battles outside.

I remember one day which was my worst day at school and – in a way – it was also my best. I had this new blouse which was so nice. I was very pleased with it and when Mum said I could wear it to school, I felt so proud. It was white and had lace on it. The blouse was really beautiful and it felt nice, so smooth against the skin. I felt flash in this blouse. When I went into school, these boys all ganged up and got an ink well and picked it up. There was a way of putting a ruler next to an ink well and catapulting the ink well and they catapulted this ink all over me. My whole blouse was ruined, it became a blue and white blouse. I was so mad I started to cry. I thought, You wait until we get out and I'll kill you. I got in the playground and waited for one of the boys and when I got hold of him, I would not let go. I nearly killed that kid! I thought I would get my own back that way. The others all ganged up and made a plan that they would get me that evening. So as soon as school finished, I knew I was in for it. I knew they were going to get me. I was coming up to fifteen then. I came out the school gates and they were all following me. All the girls were looking and I thought they were going to kill me – what was I going to do? I started to walk along. The further I walked the longer they followed me and those kids were getting closer and closer. I was really scared. I didn't know what to do, what was going to happen, and then this Irishman came along. He must have assessed the situation and realized what was happening. Well, he got to me first. He came up to me and said, 'It's all right, Girlie.' I was literally shaking because I knew they were going to kill me. There was my whole class and much of the school was behind them. All of a sudden this guy got hold of me and turned me to the kids and said,

'Look at her!' I was really tiny for my age. He said, 'You want to lay a finger on her, do it now, because I tell you, you are not going to get away with it.' The kids started saying, 'Well, who are you, are you her dad?' And he said, 'Yes, I'm her dad!' And they were shocked. They were shocked! They had never actually seen my dad or my mum and here was my dad and he was a white man. Oh dear, could you imagine that? The shock of it! They all said, 'Is that your dad, is this your dad?' I was so frightened I couldn't talk. And he kept saying, 'Yes, I'm her dad and I'm telling you, you lay off of her, don't make me come up the school for any of you. If any of you hits her, I'll know about it.' And then he actually walked me near home. At that time, I didn't think of any dangers (like him running off with me) because it didn't happen the way it does now. But I was so pleased and proud of this man. Oh my God, I then wished my father was white! I really wished he was white. I knew there and then that people were going to be all right to me and from that day everyone in the school became my friend. Everyone in the class was my friend because they had the thought that my dad was white. Until the day I left, I never ever let on that he wasn't.

There were subjects that I did well at in the West Indies, but to come to the London way of teaching, I felt as though I was backwards. The teaching was not the same and my progress was not the same. I had always excelled at English in the West Indies. I always carried straight A's. When I came here, I would be given a C or minus this or minus that, and I didn't understand why English wasn't the same wherever you were. The pronunciations even now are quite different between, say, an English person and an American or West Indian. I couldn't understand this. I hated maths but algebra was something I spent a lot of time studying in Barbados and I could do it, but in London they didn't teach algebra. So, I felt they were not teaching me what I was used to learning. To do money, I had to revert from shillings and dollars to florins and shillings and pounds because that was the coinage of the day – thruppence and sixpence! It was complicated and I had to learn a whole new way of using money.

Well, I had all this aggro at school and when I came home there was no one to listen to my point of view. When my parents came home, I was asleep. My mum would always come and wake me up and I would get up and help her because she would then prepare the dinner for the following day. She would be up in the mornings at about five o'clock, cooking. Weekends were a disaster. I remember on Saturdays, Mum would go round the markets. She loved them. So I would always be hauled around these markets. If it was a market, that was my mum's place and she loved it. Most of all from where we lived, we went to the one in Edgware Road. That was her favourite. Mum liked to collect china and specially brass, which she loved very much. Up to now, you can look around my house and you will not see a piece of brass! Old jewellery she bought, she loved that – anything bric-a-brac. But mostly, she would buy her vegetables and foodstuffs there. We would start off in the morning and we would end up with about forty bags, pulling them and struggling to get everything back. She was a great one for walking. She would walk and I would be tagging along with all these bags with her. Now I will go in a market once in a while if someone else is going or if I am going for something specific, but I detest markets and I detest brass because I ended up cleaning it. Those days that would start off very early in the morning and finish late in the evening! At six o'clock we would just be getting home.

Once indoors, it was then the ritual of cleaning the house. Although Mum had tenants, she always had the opinion that no one looks after your house like you do, you couldn't expect tenants to. As I said, she was one for cleanliness. In those days, lino was the floor-covering. They used to do a special lino which was red and had a little diamond-shaped pattern to it with underfelt beneath and it was hard-wearing. That was throughout all the landings and on the stairways. I used to have to get a scrubbing brush and water and get it cleaned before the water went cold in the bucket. I scrubbed each stair and then washed it off. And then I waxed it all with the polish. I waxed it because it had to shine! And that was my job. This I had to do every Saturday from the time I came here. It took about an hour and a half, but at the time it seemed like for ever.

While I was doing the lino, Mum would be putting away all the shopping she had bought. At the same time, she would be having all these pans of water heating up to soak the laundry. She is fanatical about washing. She would never wash white clothes with coloured clothes so the laundering was all done in sections. All the white delicate clothes would be washed separately, the other whites would be soaked and scrubbed. If my mum did a shirt, you would think it was brand new out of a shop. Today, this is the business that they have – their main business is a laundry. My dad was a tailor by profession but there was not enough money in making suits. He used to make suits for Burtons. It was nothing for him to run up five hundred suits a week. And in between, if anyone wanted a suit, he would tailor that suit. He was very very good at it. Then he started doing special suits for bespoke tailors. But he still couldn't make as much as working on the railways. Once he started working on the railways, he would do his employed job and still do the sewing. Dad had these big Singer sewing-machines, two of them. Certain cloths were put on each machines. My parents took them back to the West Indies.

My mum was always good at pressing. If she pressed a shirt it would never have a crease or a wrinkle. Although they own a laundry, so fanatical is my mum that her clothes are never done in a machine. Her clothes are all done by hand and she does them herself. All my dad's shirts are perfection. At the time, I didn't think anything about all this laundry – it was just Mum's way. I didn't question the way that she was.

But there are certain things I have learned from my mum that I have tried not to inherit. Take Christmas, for instance. Christmas is a big time for all families in any country. There would always be new curtains for Christmas but those curtains would never be hung till about five o'clock Christmas morning because everything had to be new. No neighbours ever saw our new curtains until they opened their own curtains on Christmas Day and looked at our house. There would be a new tablecloth, the food would have to be prepared. Since everything was done on Christmas Eve, you never slept that night. The turkey would have to be stuffed and seasoned and there would be ham. Mum never baked the cake until then. Today, it is the same thing in the West Indies. Mum still has not got out of the habit. And I can't stand that! My cakes will be done a week or two before. I change my curtains but they are done earlier. There is no way I am waiting till Christmas Eve. Christmas Eve, I want to relax and have a nice time with the family and sit down and talk or even go out and know that it is all done. I like the English way. I have settled into it. I remember those old times as being such hard times and I wouldn't want them to happen to my children. Even though I am now grown up, it is hard when I go home and I see my mum struggling, still doing things the hard way. You know there is no way you can say, 'Well, there is an easier way to do this.' This is the way she has always done it, this is her way, her method, and her way is *the way*.

You didn't find West Indian food as readily as now but you did get it in the markets. Mum didn't use a lot, though. When I first came the food was not what I had been used to. There would always be two or three veg on the table when we sat down to dinner although there would be rice as well. There was always salad and potatoes, either mashed, boiled, baked or chips. I used to like chips. But although having fish and chips on a Friday night is the norm, if we had it during the week chips wouldn't be classed as a proper meal. Friday night it was an easy thing while during the week, if you had chips you had to have other dishes with it. My parents would not eat baked beans or egg, chips and beans. As a young girl growing up having my own kids, I enjoyed eating baked beans with them! I think most older West Indians wouldn't consider beans or chips as a proper meal.

On Saturday, after the stairs, there were other chores I could do. In our sitting room, we had a carpet – not a fitted one – but a square where you could see the lino around the edges. First, I had to sweep the lino and then wash and polish it. Although no one had been in that sitting room for the whole week, it would have collected dust and would have to be done. And then I had to brush the carpet. This dreaded red carpet could only be brushed one way. It was very expensive and was also shipped to the West Indies because my parents paid so much money for it. It was very plush. We didn't have a hoover so I used to use a hand brush. I used to get down on my hands and knees and clean this carpet and I dreaded it because once it was cleaned, even if you just rested your hand on it, it left a mark. You couldn't really touch it. The sitting room was Mum's pride and joy because she had this brass and the china and there would be all this lace in tablecloths hanging around, all nicely pressed. When you went in, it looked very plush but what work went in to get it that way! I hated that carpet. All the time I have had fitted carpets for me and my kids, I have never had a red carpet. Once I got married, I rebelled and decided all the things I had done all my life I wouldn't do any more.

It was very late when we finished on Saturday and what wasn't finished on the Saturday was finished off on Sunday. I didn't mind Sundays so much because Sunday was the only day that the radio went on in the house. We were able to hear stories on the radio. I used to get involved in the serials. Every week, I would tune in to *Paul Temple*. This was an intriguing series and it used to always be, 'Who Killed This Person!' Mum and I listened, but not Dad. By the time he finished working, he would just lie down and go to sleep. *Paul Temple* used to come on at half past seven to eight o'clock. That was the night I had my big bath: my hair was washed and plaited and all those things. Sometimes we didn't have dinner until very late what with all the cleaning and ironing. What Mum used to do was wet the clothes, damp them, and then iron them. She had an electric iron and it would do the job all right but it wasn't a steam iron. Mum got a big sheet and put the damped clothes in that and folded them up. Once they were in the sheet, they stayed damp until you took them out to iron them.

We didn't have a fridge. I don't think my parents had a fridge until they went home in 1961. Everything was kept in the larder. You didn't have a fitted kitchen like now. You used to have a cupboard, actually, and there would be shelves to keep things on. The window-sills were a lot bigger than in new houses today. When Mum made a jelly, that went out on the window-sill. Everything went into plastic bags and went outside. Or a chicken, if it was cooked and you had leftovers, that was kept outside on the window-sill. Mum had an option of two window-sills. In the front of the house there was a window-box which you couldn't stand on but you could put flowers in. It was deep. If you opened the sitting-room window, you could put stuff in this box and it would keep fresh and cold. So that was Mum's fridge.

My neighbourhood was mostly white though there were a couple of coloured people in it. In those days, you didn't see a great deal of coloured, and if we saw someone coloured we would always feel pleased. If they were living on the same street, my parents would have known them and they would have said hello and known what work each other did. There was a coloured family living across the road with about five daughters. They had a telly! I used to try and hurry up and get my work done so I could go and see *Bonanza* which was on mid-week. There was one girl my age. We didn't go to the same school but we left at the same time in the morning and we used to talk things over. Her school always seemed a lot better than my school, so when my brother and sister arrived in this country my parents sent them to Aylestone and they got on well and everyone was very pleased. But by the time my brother and sister arrived, there were a lot more coloured children. When I left school, there were quite a lot of coloured children around.

I felt, well, the whites were not like us. My mum had a lot of English friends and people from Selfridges would come to tea. It was always a big elaborate affair when they came. We would have cucumber sandwiches with no crusts and special cakes, all different, and the best china. Oh, dear, it was such an elaborate thing! I would have to sit and be lady-like. Sometimes my mum and myself would go back to these people for tea. My dad didn't socialize a lot at all. In the time that my parents came, a lot of other black people came as well and they exchanged addresses. Kilburn and the Harrow Road and Portobello Market were places where they used to meet. Sometimes on Saturdays, Dad used to go to Portobello and would meet the coloured people who more or less all lived locally. We had friends living in Brondesbury and we used to walk from where we lived to go and see these friends. I told you my mum liked walking! There were people around that Dad knew. Even a few years ago when he came over, he retraced his steps of those early days but it had changed quite a lot. Till today, he doesn't drink and doesn't smoke. He has never been into a pub and never wanted to. That's my dad. Politics were never discussed in my house. I don't think either of my parents ever voted. They didn't seem to be interested but it was not something you would pick up on anyway as a kid.

Mum never smoked and doesn't like it. My sister has a cigarette now and again, one day a week. I smoke though. I think my first introduction to cigarettes was when I was at school because after the incident with the Irish chap, I was accepted into the gang. The boys and girls used to say, 'Her father's white!' I was always hearing that. I was then invited to their homes. So all the sixth-formers would come out and we would have our pocket money and go down to the chip shop and buy chips. Some of the girls lived very close to school and we would go back to their houses to smoke and drink pop. Because we were sixth-formers, we would bunk off school and change into swimsuits. We would look at each other's bodies and everyone realized I was no different to them, the only difference being that I was black and they were white. But there was no physical difference. I think then we were 'all girls together'. They all had their eyes on which boy they liked but personally I wasn't into boys. I don't think I was ready for knowing about boys up until I left school. I just wasn't that way inclined yet.

My mum and I would sometimes go to the cinema on a Saturday night, just me and my mum. We would go to see Jerry Lewis and any Frank Sinatra film or the Bing Crosby and Bob Hope movies. Mum liked comedy. I don't think we ever went to the theatre, though. Actually, I was hooked on Jerry Lewis. When I became pregnant, I would go to the cinema and watch Jerry Lewis films all the time. You see, at the mother and baby home all the girls there used to smoke and talk about the outrageous things they had done. I used to just sit and think to myself, Well, they've had boyfriends, they have been out, they know what it is all about! Why am I here? I didn't do anything! The thought of what those girls got up to! They were meeting boys outside and I didn't do any of that. I just couldn't understand it. I wasn't bad so why was I there? All those girls smoked. After that I would never buy cigarettes. The time I really started smoking was after my kids were all born. That's when I started having a cigarette again.

I didn't have much of a life which was why I was so glad to get out to work because I was then able to see people and how they lived. My first job at fifteen and a half was at Addressograph Multigraph Limited in Willesden. They used to print plates and these plates would have to be cleaned. I don't remember my exact job there. I know I had to handle a lot of these plates but I didn't do the printing. It could be I did something with testing and packing. Then my parents tried very hard to get me into a good occupation. They really went out of their way. My dad wanted me to go and be a seamstress because he was a tailor but I was not interested in the least and said so. Mum took me around many days in the West End because she worked there. We went to a shop making hats and I looked round. In those days it was different than now because people would let you come in and see how the other people were working and what sort of environment you would be working in. You didn't just meet the staff in a receptionist capacity, you actually went onto the shop floor and saw the work being done. I went to numerous places, all down in Soho. At that time, there were lots of factories and it was not as notorious as it is now. There were lots of different things going on down there, like film companies, and we went into all of them. And then my parents said, 'You like cooking so perhaps you should go and try the catering trade.'

I settled eventually for being a trainee manageress in the Lyon's Corner House at the corner of Marble Arch. It was very very nice and those were happy days, brilliant days. I was the junior and so I hardly did any work. Everyone took me under their wing. It was a rule that the juniors were entitled to longer breaks. We were given two pints of milk a day, in the morning at elevenses to feed us up and in the afternoon. We were given cakes at tea-time. Lunch-time, our meals were free and we had a choice. So it was really very nice. The people I worked with were very friendly. And in Lyon's Corner Shops you used to get a nice class of people coming in. I started at the bottom of course, waiting on tables, cleaning up, then I progressed to behind the counter. When Marble Arch was going to close we had to leave and I was transferred to the Lyons in Harlesden so that was nearer home. It was right by the Jubilee Clock in Willesden. When I go past there now I try to see the clock and remember those days. I don't think there are any Lyons shops around any more. But the cream cakes and tea trolley that went round!

When my parents left the West Indies, they didn't get any of our relatives to look after us because Mum and her parents had fallen out and apparently she was the black sheep of her family. Mum had life very hard and had to work for everything she ever wanted. When my grandfather died, he had left money for my mum in trust but her mother never gave it to her because she never liked her. All the money went to the others while Mum had to work. So while her sisters and everyone else was well-off in the family, Mum was poor. And when she went back home and actually started her business and worked and got it going, her and my dad, and became rich – rich, so like in 1972 they made their first million – it was about that time that all the family realized she was better off than all of them. In the end, it was my mum who paid for my grandmother to be taken into a private nursing home and cared for because none of the family would have her and Mum was the last person my grandmother saw. But my grandmother never did anything for my mum, she just didn't like her. It was sad. My mum talks about it now and the hard upbringing and how hard life was. I feel the same! I think she wasn't told about the facts of life either. She married my dad when she was nineteen and he was in the army. He actually fought for England in the War. I feel that she could have looked at her life and realized what had happened to her was happening all over again and have acted differently, but she didn't see it, she just didn't see it, so it made my life hell in a way. I try now not to let anything, anything at all that happened when I was a child, happen to my family. Like when I was a child, my mum was never at home and my dad wasn't rich enough to buy me toys. I had no toys or dolls. Anything I had was something I made myself. You just had to make your own entertainment. So I came along and was going to buy as many toys as I could, whether new or secondhand, for my children. I made sure they had toys. And television. I never barred my kids from television because I remember that longing and the frustration of not being able to have it.

So, when my parents left for England, they paid a lady to look after us. It started off very nice as she looked after us very well indeed. My mum had got a house and we all lived there but there was lots of room and after a few months the lady brought her sister in with her. Her sister and I didn't get on although we were the same age. There were all these rows between the sister and myself. Things were a lot cheaper in England than in the West Indies and Mum would get these clothes to send to us in parcels. She would send everything you could think that we wanted to wear. When these parcels came, we would be given a dress or two and the rest went to the lady's sisters, the one living with us and others at her home. Everyone was given something from this parcel and what wasn't given away was sold. So we never got everything that was sent for us. And the money from my parents, this woman used to say it didn't arrive! It did and we knew she was getting it. Eventually Mum would send money to friends as well so that we would get pocket money and be able to buy things like other children. When Mum's friends used to see us, they would be giving us fifty cents here or a dollar there.

I don't think my parents regret for a minute having lived in England and the way things have worked out. It helped them to achieve something in life and set them up, a stepping-stone. My dad more or less said that when they were interviewed on *Whicker's World* as people who had come to England, achieved something and returned home. For me, I am pleased at Dad's success but at the same time I feel I was sacrificed to this ambition. I don't think I could live in Barbados now because my life was unsettled then and I don't really remember a great deal about it coming here so young. It was such a different way of life. Everything for me really happened here: growing up and having my children, getting married, working, getting divorced, remarrying, having a home. Everything happened here. I couldn't really say, 'Yes, I could pick myself up and go home to live.' I would need something drastic to change my whole life for this to happen.

The only things I have kept and treasured from my childhood aren't toys, but clothes. When I grew up, I realized those early clothes my parents gave me were the sort of clothes that lasted. If my dad made a suit, that suit would be such a classic that any time you wear it, it would always look fresh and well made and it would hang well. So these clothes were what I treasured. I liked dresses, hats, handbags and gloves. I had gloves to match my outfits, lacy gloves as well. I was very careful with my clothes because that was the way I was brought up. I actually have some of my clothes from my teens that Mum bought me – even throughout all my children I have kept my figure and can still get into them. So I have these clothes to last me a lifetime. They go out of fashion and come back in again and I pass some on to my daughter, although she never treats them or respects them in the way that I do. I still have the dress that I wore to my wedding reception when I got married the first time in 1962. If I showed it to you now, you would not believe that I have kept that dress for all these years because it looks as fresh as today. It was from Selfridges, of course.

With Mum and Dad, I dare say that, as prosperous as they were, they didn't really over-indulge in things here. The reason for that is because they had made the plans they were going to go home and start a business of their own. They did send for my brother and sister, though. They came in 1960 and didn't go back home with Mum and Dad. When Mum realized she was pregnant again and my brother and sister had just come, she placed my brother with foster parents. This lady looked after him because he really didn't want to go back to Barbados again. He was about fourteen or fifteen at the time.

I, by this time, had given birth to my son in 1960. I had become bored with the loneliness and one of the lodgers and I got involved. I remember that my parents were so busy paying attention to their work they didn't have time for me, and this lodger showed me affection and attention. One thing led to another. I was told practically nothing about sex. Only, if you let any man do anything to you, you are going to get pregnant! But I really didn't know what *anything* was. From school, I realized enough to know that once a penis went into you that was it, you were going to get pregnant. And when it actually happened that very first time, I fell pregnant. This was in 1959 and it was the turning-point of my life. There was my mum and dad who thought their lives were all planned out and they were going home and all the rest of it, and I was working, and my sister and my brother were about to come, and then I did this. I didn't know I was pregnant and they didn't know I was pregnant, either. I kept being sick in the mornings, feeling queasy, and then I would be all right. I wasn't too bad. So I continued going to work but by this time I didn't like the new Lyons they had sent me to in Harlesden and had gone to work in a laundry. Still being a junior, they more or less looked after me. I was putting on some weight and my mum sent me down to the doctor. I was very tiny, I was still so tiny. The doctor said it could be indigestion and I needed to go on a diet. That could easily have been when I was about four months. The funny thing was I had only ever had one period and I was frightened when I had had it because Mum had never discussed that sort of thing with me. I had been too scared to tell her when my period started. At first, I didn't know what it was. When I realized, it only lasted a day or two and that was it. When I didn't see it again, I was worried, but not worried enough. I thought, Great! It was dirty anyway, I didn't like this thing. Mum had a white bag with all the sanitary stuff in it. If I ever needed any, I knew where to go. So that was that. Nobody told me it was a normal part of growing up. I just used what I wanted from the bag and there was always plenty left over.

Of course, the bed had a big mark in it from when I lost my virginity. I turned the mattress over because I didn't want my parents to think that I had done something bad. You were made to think that men were so bad and evil. I don't think for one minute Mum or Dad could have thought anything would have happened with one of the lodgers. When I continued to not lose any weight, Mum decided she would take me to the doctor herself and the doctor actually did a urine test and sent Mum with me to the hospital. When the doctor told her I was six months pregnant, she fell off the chair! I was more scared of what happened to her than I was about what the doctor said to me. Then she started to cry and asked who it was and I started to cry as well and sobbed, 'I didn't do anything!' I can laugh about this now but for a long time it was a part of my life I didn't want to talk about. It was only after I went and took counselling and tried to do counselling myself that I was actually able to come to terms with this. It was awful.

What happened then was my parents called in the police because I was under age. It was dreadful. After the constant pressure, I had to say who it was. This lodger actually had money. At the time I didn't know it and didn't look to him for anything. He knew that my parents were always out, he knew that there was no one there, he knew the situation and he took advantage. He was put on remand in prison and got himself a very good lawyer. This man told the solicitors that I was asking him for money and that I knew he was rich and soon everybody was on his side. It was very bad the way they all were shouting at me. He told the solicitors that my parents were always running after me at night, that I would never come home.

My parents were not prepared to spend any money on me. In fact, from within a few days of them knowing I was pregnant and knowing what I had done, I was sent away to Chiswick to a mother and baby home. The disgrace of it all! Me, to get pregnant, the shame of it! And nobody thought about me at all. They only thought of the shame I had brought on the family and what the neighbours would say. They had to get me out of the way. So I was hurriedly packed off to this mother and baby home run by the Salvation Army. And from that day until the day I appeared in the Old Bailey, I never saw my parents. I kept writing to them and Mum and Dad would never answer my letters. They had to wait until after the baby was born for the trial.

Mum and Dad probably just didn't know how to handle the situation and did so very badly. I have since spoken to my mother about this time and she actually said if she had her life to live all over again, she would not make that mistake again. She realized afterwards and she was sorry, but at the time she just handled it to the best of her abilities.

When I got into the court, for the life of me I don't think

I said one word. The place was so huge. To me, it was an enormous building. There were all these people looking at me and all these men with white wigs, and there was me with this little baby that I couldn't even have normally – they had to do a caesarean section. Throughout all this, I couldn't even see my parents and even when my baby was born I got nothing at all, I was totally isolated. I refused to give up my baby for adoption. He was mine, he was the first real thing that I actually had for me and I was pleased that I had this child. My first child is now big and he's good and I like him a lot. But the injustice of this situation really hit me.

It was true that I often wasn't in at night. Because my parents were never there anyway, I would want to be with friends. And I didn't get involved with any boys or anything like that but there was this English girl who belonged to the Salvation Army and I used to go around with her. We used to get out and sing 'Onward Christian Soldiers' and I had the tambourine and used to bang it! I was really enjoying all this but my parents were thinking I was doing other things. Of course, at first they thought I would be involved with boys rather than with the Church. They actually followed me and found out that it was not the church they belonged to – they were Church of England. There was me visiting a Salvation Army church! It was just not heard of! So I was made to stop going. This was when all my problems started because I didn't have anything else to do. But they didn't see it like that at the time. Of course, the lodger got off. I don't really know what happened in the end but I do know that the trauma of the courtroom was an experience such that until today I don't like any courts. I think if I was ever called up in a court for any reason I would have a heart attack. That is the phobia I have got about it. I feel very bad even if I read a case where some young person is involved at the Old Bailey. I remember my experience there and I feel sympathetically towards the person who is being charged but no sympathy for the prosecution because I feel the way they treat young people is really very bad. At the court was the first time

I'd seen my parents since they'd sent me away and when they saw that child they were overwhelmed by him and didn't want me to go back to the mother and baby home. Within a few weeks I moved back home.

Looking back on the whole episode of getting pregnant, I remember thinking to myself that something more had to happen than actually did. As quick as it was there, *he* was there, it was over. And I didn't feel anything. I didn't reach a climax or enjoy it. I didn't know how to have foreplay or anything. It was just *bam*, pregnant! And after I got back home with the baby, there was no peace because I was hearing the disgrace of it every minute.

# STEPHANIE

I don't really know why my parents decided to emigrate to New Zealand. I think Dad was a bit discontented after the War. He had been quite active in the navy, had been on the Malta convoy and the Russian convoy, and his ship had been sunk – torpedoed. He was then shipwrecked and had a long march through the desert to get to Alexandria. It was a case of being rescued in the nick of time. He told us all about how he marched across the desert and apparently it really was true. Now, my father has never spoilt a good story for the sake of telling the truth, but once he would have given anything for a glass of water as they had run out, and he spat out his false teeth because they were taking up all the moisture in his mouth. Just over the brow of the next sand dune they saw this army camp so he ran back and retrieved his false teeth! The biggest disappointment that he can remember was when they got to the army camp they'd run out of water too, and all they had was beer. He said he would have given anything just for a glass of nice cool water but they had to have army beer.

So when he came back after the War I suppose he was a bit run-down and miserable. My mother said apparently he came home one day and gave her three choices: South Africa, South America or New Zealand. He could transfer to one of their navies because they needed teachers, instructors. And he said, 'Pick one, because we are not staying here'. She opted for New Zealand because the lifestyle would be most similar to our life in England.

From what I can remember, our neighbourhood in Southsea was quite nice. We had our own home although there was a sitting-tenant upstairs, a Miss Hurley, who went with the house. It was the same as now. When you bought a house and there was a tenant you had to buy the house with the tenant in it. And she was a dreadful old woman. She used to come halfway down the stairs and pull faces at us: really potty. She would never get out of her dressing gown, which was made of dreadful old pink flannel, and her hair was a mess. She looked like a wicked witch. My sister, Sandra, and I were fascinated. We used to stand at the bottom of the stairs and she would be pulling all these awful faces at us. We would just stand there looking up at her, not frightened even though she was quite a horrific sight. I remember we used to go on walks to the common and along South Parade Pier, where they had illuminations in those days. I didn't feel deprived or anything. We saw no signs of hardship, but then, my mother was very much into sacrificing for us both and we never realized that there were shortages at all.

There are photos of me along South Parade Pier. Everybody tells me what a pretty child I was. I mean by this: my aunts, my uncles, my parents. But I really feel that they are biased. Looking at photos of me, I think I am all right but the fact is Mum lost a daughter before she had me and she didn't have me until after the War in '46. She had to have an operation which cost her a hundred pounds – quite a sum in those days. Her womb was tilted or something. And I suppose it was just the effort and everything involved to have me that made me wonderful in her family's eyes, although everyone else was probably very fed up hearing about this oncoming child. I had tight curly hair, very Shirley Templeish and it was red. As it was naturally tight, I remember the agony I had to go through when it was brushed. Oh, I used to cry before she started just to look at the hairbrush! And she was very kind, my mother. She would never do anything to hurt me. But of course we didn't have conditioner in those days. Think of how much easier it would have been with conditioner.

It was 1953 and I was seven when we finally left for New Zealand. We delayed it for quite a long time, actually, for the best part of a year, because my sister got chicken-pox. We missed the original sailing and there were sailings only once every six or eight months. The boat we were originally meant to go on was apparently full of ten-pound assisted-passage people but the one we went on later, the *Rangitoto*, was quite luxurious.

I can remember we had the choice of all this wonderful food and there was a nurse looking after us most of the time. My father had gone on ahead and it was just my mother and us kids. She used to be out just about every night, dancing and doing I don't know what, and all I can remember is her bending over us with a rustle of taffeta and the sparkle of her artificial diamond necklace, smelling so nice and saying good night. She really did look very nice.

I was very curious about her outings in the evening and I used to go up and spy on her. Sandra wouldn't come initially so I used to go up on my own. I used to put my dressing-gown on over my nightie and would go up on deck. The dance floor had these big square windows situated on the deck and you could look in. It was like a scene out of Evelyn Waugh – everybody there, all the women in their beautiful dresses, smoking cigarettes out of cigarette-holders. The men wore dinner-jackets and I can remember kissing hands seemed to be the 'in' thing. There I would spy my mother wafting around the dance floor. It was rather fun, I didn't mind. And then I persuaded Sandra to come up with me. This went on for quite some time until about four weeks out of England my mother happened suddenly to look up. She must have been standing near the windows and she saw these two faces looking in at her. Of course that spoiled her evening! And from then on in, I suppose, it spoiled her evenings because she never knew when she was going to look up and see these two faces pressed up against the glass looking in at her.

I was a right little nark and told my father. When we got to New Zealand, he met us in Wellington and one of the first things I told him was that I had met my 'uncle' on board ship but I knew he wasn't my uncle. This man came up and introduced himself and said he was my uncle so-and-so. And I said, 'Well, you're not my uncle! I know you're not my uncle.' Then there was a silence. So I told Dad about it and all he did was laugh. I remember thinking even as a child, 'This isn't right. My mother

113

shouldn't really be doing these sort of things.' We felt very possessive of our mother!

After Dad met us, we got on the train. Since we were so well cared for I can't remember feeling cold or tired or anything. In those days in New Zealand, the trains looked like cattle trucks which is what they were basically. They had no carriages like they had in England. There wasn't a buffet car or refreshments at all. And what used to happen was they would go along so many miles and then stop at a station. Everybody would rush out as fast as they could, queue up at the station buffet, and come in loaded with New Zealand Rail thick mugs of tea and curled-up sandwiches. It was a real fight to get anything and you had to take the mugs back before the train left so it was very uncomfortable and very unpleasant. Anyway, the porter came round and he asked Mum if we had just arrived and Mum said, 'Yes', and he then asked if the little girls would like anything. He said he could get us some hot milk. He was obviously going to go back to his van and heat the milk up for us. And I turned to him imperiously and asked, 'What *else* have you got?' Mum said she could have fallen through the floor! The poor man was being kind and going out of his way.

The first thing we did when we got 'home' was to take our shoes off and run around on the stones. My father said that in New Zealand nobody wears shoes and we children would have to get our feet toughened up. So we made a point of this. The house itself was falling around our ears. It was a rented house and all the net curtains were in tatters. There was no hot water. Mum had to heat everything up in the boiler. We had to stand in a tub in the laundry to be washed at night and it was awful. All the conditions were so primitive compared to what we were used to in England.

Dad eventually bought a run-down old villa house in Auckland and proceeded to do it up. But of course then he was sent off to Korea and my mother was left in this house, which was in a dreadful state. Birds used to poke their heads in through the ceiling and even though it was not as cold as England, the wind in the winter used to whistle through. It was pretty awful for my mother but as children we didn't worry about it at all. My mother spent a lot of time crying. My main memory of that time is she was always secretly in tears. There was never a big hysterical outburst but there were tears rolling down her face all the time, poor woman. It must have been awful for her. We had a big garden, a quarter-acre, and she used to mow that with a hand-mower. Gardens in Auckland, which is almost sub-tropical, aren't like here where nothing grows for so many months. They grow all the year round. I can understand why she must have been in tears. She often says if they had money then she would have turned around and gone home. Of course she was very homesick.

The New Zealanders had a bit of resentment about the immigrants coming to their country but Mum and Dad's friends were mainly from the English navy who had been sent out with Dad, so my parents didn't lack for friendship. I remember at school I wasn't very popular, nor was my sister, simply because we were English. It seemed to be that the New Zealanders rented their homes, they never thought to buy them. The English would come over, work hard and save their money, and buy a home and this was held in much resentment by the New Zealanders. I think my parents did very well because they were probably used to scrimping and saving, coming from England and not having the money.

I'm never sure about what 'class' we were but we had everything we wanted. My mother wanted more for us than she had had. She used to try to push us and took us along to this expensive, exclusive tennis club. My sister and I were both fairly good at tennis. Sandra stayed on but I went once or twice and found them all a bit too much – snobby – and I didn't go again. I used to go off in my tennis whites with my tennis racquet and sit in the milk bar for a couple of hours or however long we would ordinarily play tennis. Then I'd wander home as if I'd played a match at the tennis club. I think she was trying to apply standards that were relative in England at the time. In New Zealand these weren't really applicable.

Dad being in the navy, there were a lot of functions they attended. There were always balls and parties. My mother always looked lovely in a dress that she had made and Dad was very handsome in his navy uniform. My mother sold most of the furniture we had in England and I think she regretted that. We only brought really personal stuff. But we were very smart compared to the kids in New Zealand.

My mother was an excellent dressmaker. She had done a tailoring course and sewed for us and made herself suits and things which were very fashionable in those days. We had nice clothes. I think there was a bit of envy between the mothers of the children we were friendly with. They always used to admire our clothes but at that age, of course, we didn't realize, we didn't care what we wore. It was all to do with what we were comfortable wearing. I know that there was always someone who wanted our cast-offs that Mum had made. I remember even when I got to about twenty she would point across the road and say, 'Stephanie, there's that coat I made for you when you were such-and-such an age!', and I can't remember the coat but she would have done. She used to do beautiful things like inset velvet collars, all bound, so I suppose they went on and on being worn by various people and passed on. They never seemed to wear out.

In New Zealand, we all lived on quarter-acre sections and everybody plonked their home in the middle of their quarter-acreage and there were lots of trees and fruit trees. There were masses of children. My father had bought us bikes and mechanical toys and dolls on various trips he had been on to Singapore. He was with the New Zealand navy at that point and we were out riding our bikes, exploring, doing the Famous Five thing! Of course, in those days everybody read *The Famous Five* and we used to enact the stories. We backed onto a creek which was overgrown with lots of oak trees and secret places and it was a real wonderland for children. All your imagination could run riot and you could play Cowboys and Indians or Princesses.

We used to go to the pictures on Saturday afternoons and we would always come back and play out the films. These were films like *The Princess of the Nile* and *The Black Knight* and, of course, the goodie always overcame the baddie. There would always be a beautiful woman and among the girls there would always be a fight over who should play the princess. There were two prima donnas in our group and these two girls, Cheryl Coleman and Pamela Godley, used to preen themselves and say, 'Well, if I can't be the princess, then I am going home!' And we would all rally round and say, 'No, don't go home. Look, Cheryl, you were the princess last week so Pamela can be her this week', and that would placate them. We played boys and girls together, the whole neighbourhood. It was quite a nice time growing up.

It seemed in those days that the weather was always warm. Still, my mother says that she doesn't even remember winter for at least three years after she was there, not that there wasn't one, it was just she said that her blood was so thick being used to the English winter that she didn't recognize winter when it arrived. So I suppose we were the same. And it never influenced us as far as going out was concerned. It used to rain and was a bit cooler but it never was weather like you got in England where it was so bad you didn't want to go out in the cold. The winters were very mild.

New Zealand had rationing after the War, but I can't remember it. Even when we were in England, I don't remember not having things like chocolate biscuits or chocolate. Mum used to buy a bar of chocolate once a week in England and we would all sit around while she would read to us on a Sunday afternoon and dole out this chocolate, share it out between us all. That was a real event – Sunday afternoons, a story and the chocolate. And I can remember the Italian ice-cream man who used to ride by in England. I don't remember war damage although there must have been lots in Southsea because of the port of Portsmouth.

There were always all sorts of government restrictions on things in New Zealand because, of course, they hadn't got the wealth of England. All New Zealand had was their primary produce and they hadn't got the income that Britain had, so that everything was a luxury, all the things we were used to having, even in post-war England. In those days, my mother, I think, quite resented it. I mean in England she could set her mind on something, buy the material, envisage the pattern or buy, say, a piece of bias binding in the colour she wanted. She used to be able to go down the road and get it and in New Zealand she couldn't. What she ended up doing was making her own bias binding. It was quite bad in those days. It was even bad when I was married, so it must have been dreadful in the Fifties. And it was then that there were all the tears.

We had a radio but no TV. When I was about thirteen the girl across the road, Cheryl (one of the prima donnas who always wanted to be princess), got a television. Her father was an electrician and they were the first in the street to get one, so we all piled over to watch it. That was 1960 when TV first came to New Zealand, and there was only one channel. I can remember watching television in England. We didn't own one, but my aunt did. We stayed in Liverpool with her and my grandmother before we left to go to New Zealand and I can remember watching it there. So when it finally came to New Zealand, it wasn't such a novelty to me as I had seen it before. The reason the New Zealand government gave to explain why they couldn't have television earlier was the mountains. I can't see why there was a problem. I think it was just their shortsightedness. It did finally get there on one channel. There are three now.

We lived in a place called Devonport. The harbour is very similar to how I imagine Sydney to be, all indented; also the main part of the city of Sydney is across a bridge and people live on what they call the North Shore. Well, we lived on the North Shore equivalent in Auckland, but when we got to New Zealand they didn't have a bridge. We used to have to go across by vehicular ferry or by just ordinary passenger ferry. The vehicular ferry took the car. You drove the car on and drove off the other side. To go to 'Town', which Auckland city was called, you had to get the bus down to the ferry, and then get on the ferry. It was a lovely trip of course. The harbour is magnificent. All the main shops were there and it is still the major shopping area. In our neighbourhood, there was a baker and a small grocery shop, the way they had them in England, where you would go and ask for things and the grocer would get them off the shelf and measure out your cheese. And there was a dairy – a milk bar they called it – where they sold milk and milk shakes and ice creams. We used to sit there and have sundaes. It was half English and half American, even then. That was just a short walk up the hill.

I can't remember playing with a lot of toys. We had our bikes and trolleys and were quite tomboyish. We used to ride round. And of course we had a lot of books from England. There was a library locally. I used to read everything, whatever I was given to read, really. We would go along and Mum would say, 'I think it is best if you read that', and I would whine, 'I really want to read this'. But she would say, 'No, no, you're not quite old enough for that, dear!' So it was all monitored, what I read. It was heavily Enid Blyton. I think this is hilarious now but I did think at the time it was very adventurous and *The Famous Five* books were my favourites. I liked them better than the *The Secret Seven*.

Being a dressmaker, my mother used to smock our dresses and we had puffed sleeves. The dresses tied in a bow at the back. I can't remember ever being restricted running around and climbing trees and things which I used to do. I guess I just used to do it in my dresses. I can't remember being bellowed at to change. I did dreadful things, I know. I can remember Mum saying, 'You've ruined your dress again with oil', because I used to go fiddling in motor-mower engines. I was horrible as a child. I used to say I didn't want any dinner and would sneak a piece of cat's meat down to the bottom of the garden and an old tin. And I would cook that scraggy meat up in this

old tin with a few chopped onions. The tin was very rusty.
I used to just like doing things like that to get away from
our civilized everyone-around-the-tea-table.

We had a cooked meal every evening with a pudding.
And a cooked breakfast. My mother started out serving us
all the same things that we had for breakfast in England.
It was usually cooked, or fried bread or something, an egg
at least. And it wasn't until I was much older that I really
got fed up with being force-fed. Of course, I love my food
and I always have and I used to generally eat what was
put in front of me. Eating wasn't a big thing in my life.
There was always food and it was put there so I would eat
it, not like my sister who had all sorts of fads and fancies
and wouldn't eat this or that. I suppose I was a bit fatter
then, too, than the average girl of my height. I finally put
my foot down and decided I wasn't going to have these
huge breakfasts and my packed lunch. I needed a suitcase
to carry it! I had everything – sandwiches, cold pastries,
bits of shepherd's pie or some other pie that she had
cooked. She used to do little puddings in little bowls. It
was just incredible. The other kids didn't have such nice
food as my sister and I and we used to swap it for comics
or marbles. We must have been real tomboys swapping the
boys our cake for marbles.

I thought boys were a bit silly at times but I did quite
like them. I didn't have any problems with them. They
used to come around and we would play together but that
is what we also did with girl-friends. We were at an age
where we didn't think of doing anything else. I was very
late developing. When I must have been about twelve, I
used to think there was something wrong with me because
all the girls in the class had their periods and they all had
breasts and here I was flat-chested. The highlight of it all
was my birthday party at twelve or thirteen. I had everyone to tea, all the locals – boys too – and one boy I was
particularly friendly with got me in a corner and tweaked
at my breasts! I was outraged! He sort of went to kiss me
and I thought, This is strange, what is he doing? because I
didn't know what he was up to. And then he just tweaked

my breasts and ran off. I just stood there nonplussed. I really didn't know what to do, I was totally unawares. We had never had sex education. My mother, I think, had left a book lying around about menstruation, hoping that we would read it. But as far as actual sex or boys and girls was concerned, well, I didn't know anything about it. I was totally amazed at his behaviour.

We were in the same form and he started leaving me presents wrapped up in paper ripped out of his exercise book. His father had his own business and so he stole the pencils from his father with the business name on them. He would wrap me up a little pencil and leave it on my desk so that when I got there in the morning there would be this little present. Another time I had a chocolate. So this went on and on. Once at the school fair he bought me a necklace. It was plastic, but I really liked being bought things. I don't remember that he tried to kiss me again.

When I was at grammar school and a bit older, fourteen, I met Greg Melville and he was the love of my life. I continued going out with him right through grammar school and I just thought he was wonderful. We used to get up to all sorts. By that I mean we used to kiss and cuddle but I wouldn't go any further, even right at the end after years of kissing and cuddling. I met him again when I was in New Zealand after years and years away. He had been out to Rhodesia and married a girl and had had a family and divorced and we met again. I felt the same feelings for him then as I had felt at school. He felt the same, too. It was just wonderful. It was just like being children all over again. Anyway, eventually we went to bed together and what a disaster! I mean, really, what a let-down after all those years. He was so vain and conceited. And battle-scarred. He had been in the army in Rhodesia and had all these dreadful tales about blowing up Africans, so I think he was a bit damaged mentally.

One day while we were sitting at school having our lunch, a girl told us all how women had babies, how they actually conceived. We were thirteen. We were too outraged and thought she was disgusting because we couldn't imagine our parents doing it and certainly couldn't imagine *the Queen* doing it. We ostracized this particular girl and didn't speak to her again for being so horrid.

The Queen was an arbiter of behaviour. She visited New Zealand around the time of the Coronation, and oh, yes, what an occasion. We had special dresses, my sister and I, red white and blue. We were so British and indoctrinated with British history and British everything. Of course Dad, being in the navy, was going to attend some sort of ceremony and we all got good seats. My mother went to town and made these dresses. They had puffed red and white gingham sleeves (sounds disastrous) and a gingham sash, and the rest was blue. They sound revolting but I don't think they were that bad, actually. On the day, we stood there and waved our Union Jacks. When the Queen was coming everybody just talked about her all the time. It was a huge topic of conversation. The Royal Family was always very important to my family and I think they were for the New Zealanders as well. Being so isolated in those days, even more so than now, the Queen coming over was such an event.

After Dad came back from Korea, we got this old Vauxhall car and we thought it was wonderful. We used to go off to various places. The car would inevitably break down or my father would get lost and he would start shouting. Then my mother would start getting all upset and Sandra and I, of course, would fight in the back seat. It was a real horror. Once we went away for a week and slept in pup tents. We had the choice of sleeping in the car or sleeping in the tent. Now sleeping in the tent might sound wonderful but even in those days I remember either your feet poked out or your head poked out and then you had all the mosquitoes. It was awful. As a child I just didn't enjoy it at all. I didn't enjoy the disagreements my parents always had about where they were going to stay, because my father being mean would drive around incessantly trying to get the best bargain. And my mother would get angry then and we would be getting hungry and tired, so it wasn't any fun. We did see a bit of New Zealand, though.

Christmas was always nice because my mother religiously maintained a traditional English Christmas. She went around scavenging – that's really what it was. All the import restrictions meant New Zealand got one load of Mackintosh Quality Street chocolates and my mother would be there rushing around asking the grocer, 'Now, when do you expect it?' And Mr Bloggs would say, 'Well, Mrs Vincent, we don't know. We are expecting it any day this week.' And she would get him to put some chocolates away. That's how it was with anything from England like that. There was only the one load of chocolates and Bassett's Liquorice All Sorts. All these things were such a treat. Initially, we got Christmas packages from our relatives in England. We used to be sent books but inevitably they would arrive too late or get lost and in the end they started sending money which wasn't quite so exciting. It was much nicer to have a present.

We never had any nostalgia about Britain at all as children as we were both crammed with patriotism and hyperbole. There were two books in our family which were almost bibles. One was called *Our Island's Story* and the other one was *Our Island's History*. One of them dealt with Boadicea and the Iceni tribes and all the ancient Britons right up until the Romans, and the other dealt with the Romans onwards, all about the Empire and things like this. Every night, we were read stories from these particular books. It is certainly not like that now. My parents are not as pro-British as they were in the old days. Obviously it must have been something to do with calming their homesickness.

My mother particularly was homesick rather than Dad. I don't think he felt much as he was the one who wanted to emigrate. She would leave New Zealand now, you know. She said other than the fact that her grandchildren are in New Zealand and that Dad wouldn't move, she would gladly come and live back here. In fact, when she recently returned she was really amazed by what she saw, she felt she had built up nicer memories. But she found she really liked England, even taking into account all the things that had gone downhill. She liked the seasons, you see, which we don't get so pronounced in Auckland and the flowers which are peculiar to England. They all grow so differently here, more regularly, whereas in New Zealand they just grow anyhow and no matter how much you try to have a regulated garden it just won't do. And she loves the countryside.

We children took New Zealand in our stride but there were some horrible things. We used to have an outside toilet. There was no such thing as an inside toilet in our neighbourhood. No matter how well-off you were you just couldn't have one because there was no sewerage system. They used to have a night-cart man come along and pick up the buckets and tip it out. And you could smell it if you were lying awake. Anyway, this outside loo used to be like a little shed with a door made of wood, and inside was a bench, which you sat on, with a big hole where you did your business into this bucket underneath. Well, this was all well and good, but there was no electricity down there, either, and you sometimes had to go down in the middle of the night. For some strange reason these insects called wetas used to frequent the loos. Why they did I do not know. But they were horrific insects and could grow to about six inches long if you included their antennae. They had huge antennae and huge back legs – all sort of barbed – and they would sit on the bench where you sat. The female was poisonous at a certain time of the year but the male wasn't, although the male was bigger. But they were nasty horrible creatures and you couldn't just squash them. What you had to do was to get a hammer and give them a good crack. They were almost scaley. We grew up and whacked wetas as a matter of course and didn't think anything of it. In the end, my mother got a potty for the night because she thought that it was a bit much to have us go down sitting on wetas in the dark!

Mum had a copper to do the laundry. Mondays was just dreadful and she would go down under the house to stoke up the copper and put all the washing in it. She used blue-bag, of course, to get the washing white. We never spoke to her on a Monday, we got to learn, because she was just out of sorts for some reason. I guess in England she sent all of our laundry out, and never had to do all that sort of thing. It was constant work over there. I can understand why she was so upset about everything. And then, of course, we got on and she got a washing-machine and it wasn't so bad, but she clung on to blue-bag for quite some time.

In the evenings we used to play cards or listen to the radio. I remember *Take it From Here* and there were loads of New Zealand quiz shows. Jack Maybury ran one of them. He was a quizmaster. There were also lots of English shows like *Paul Temple* and the *Van Dyke Affairs* with its signature tune that we all knew well. And there was *Hancock's Half Hour* which made us laugh. That was broadcast on Sundays. Sundays were a treat day. We used to have tea by the fire with toasted crumpets and sardines, goodies like cakes and things, and sit around listening to the radio. Although it wasn't cold, we used to have a fire because it was damp.

There was so much religion, too. My mother was really devoted to the Anglican Church. We used to be taken off to Sunday School every Sunday and then we also used to have to go to the family service. My mother was a Sunday School teacher as well. It all got a bit too much. I remember once coming out of the family service overhearing talk about someone's hat. It suddenly hit me what a pathetic waste of time all this was. They should be going there to worship God and there they were talking about Mrs Brown's new hat or lack of a hat and I suddenly decided that I wasn't going to go to church any more. Eventually I was allowed to get away with it because I was very unpleasant and stubborn even though I was a child. I had been confirmed by that stage and my mother thought my behaviour was rather outrageous but I just refused to go and what could they do? My father never went either so really I suppose that is what gave me the courage to stand up against going to church.

Pamela, one of the prima donnas, was a Catholic and that was viewed as being dreadful. My parents were most averse to our friendship. Dad used to tell us awful stories about Catholics: 'Now, if you ever see a nun coming, run. They capture little girls and boys and take them off.' He was speaking allegorically of course. He used to say nuns had dreadfully hairy legs under their habits and that they appeared to be nice and kind but really they were vicious. Naturally enough, I was terrified by this but I was very curious about it as well. I used to see nuns in the street but never saw any close up. Because my father had told me all this, one Saturday afternoon I made a point of going to confession with Pamela. Now, even going inside a Catholic church was a frightening experience for me because I was expecting a nun to jump out from behind some statue and grab me, but, of course, none did. I went around the Seven Stations of the Cross with Pamela and was horrified at these dreadful, gory pictures I saw. Later on, when I was a little older, I had to go into hospital to have my tonsils out. I must have been twelve and in the next bed to me was this girl who was obviously a Catholic as she used to be visited by these two nuns. Well, normally I had visitors so they all kept apart. I used to peer across at these nuns. One day they came to visit her and I didn't have any visitors so one of them came across to my bed and said, 'How are you, little girl, what's wrong with you?' And I immediately crunched up into the corner of the bed with my legs pulled up to my chest, thinking she'd come to get me! I was terrified of her and was full of fear and trembling. But even at the time when I was so frightened, I was thinking, She's not so bad after all, she's not doing anything to me, she's just being kind. My father would go on about Henry the Eighth and the rightness of *our* church. I think he was only doing it tongue-in-cheek and didn't mean it seriously. I remember my mother saying, 'Oh, for Heaven's sake, Harold, don't tell the children that sort of thing. You never know what ideas you are implanting in their heads. Do be quiet.' But of course he used to laugh. I remember him laughing and carrying on, it was just a tale like the Bogie Man. He obviously had a captive audience and liked to see us frightened by these stories.

We had a fair amount of freedom because Dad was away a lot but I remember one thing my mother hated and that was bubble gum. She thought it looked so cheap and common, people chewing bubble gum. And smoking, although we used to pinch her cigarettes and have a puff up. Both of them smoked but it was forbidden for us. We had quite a good supply of cigarettes because they never noticed a couple missing here and there. New Zealand was not built up and there were lots of cubby-holes where we used to make grass huts. There we'd indulge ourselves with chewing gum and stolen cigarettes. I remember one time when we set the bush down the back on fire through smoking. The fire brigade had to be called and all sorts of things happened. It was dreadful. No one ever found out how the fire started. They put it down to a very dry summer and the grass igniting on its own. It was really a raging inferno. We felt guilty for quite some time but when nobody twigged we knew we'd got off. It never stopped me smoking, though, and I still do.

# FLORA

My father was in the air force and it was considered more sensible for the children to stay in one school while he and my mother moved around. And so, I was sent to a convent school in Bedford in 1950. I boarded between the ages of six and seventeen when I decided to leave, declining to take my A-levels. By that time, my parents were living in France and I could go to the Sorbonne. The nuns were quite forward-looking in many ways and they got everyone through their O-levels, although I always thought if I had been to a better school I would have done more exciting things. But they had this thing about 'Careers'. 'Do you want to be a teacher or a nurse?' That was it. You were expected to do well at school but nobody gave the years beyond schooldays any thought at all. I remember one girl went to Oxford and she was absolutely fêted! That was quite amazing.

We had about three hundred girls, mostly day girls, and the boarders were at the most a hundred when I arrived. By the time I left, there were only about fifty of us in the dormitories. My grandparents lived in Bedford and my mother had been to that school which is why it was chosen for me. There were two of us who were boarders at six, and being the smallest ones, we were petted. It was really rather nice.

There was a big dormitory and a little dormitory (for big and little boarders) and as the school began to expand they turned them into classrooms and bought a couple of houses down the road for us to live in. There was lino on the floor and iron bedsteads. In the little dormitory, there were just great rows of beds. It was an enormous room and it made two or even three classrooms afterwards. They put lockers down the middle. I remember spending many happy November days there because I always used to get tonsillitis and was kept in during late autumn. The big dormitory was nice because we had separate cubicles and when you got to a 'certain' age, about eleven or twelve, you were allowed to draw your curtain. Before that you changed in the open. When you were in the little dormitory, you used to have to get undressed with your dressing-gown around your shoulders for modesty. Nobody had anything to show but everybody just did this because everyone else did!

Our school uniform was navy blue and white – a tunic with a white blouse and a tie – and when you were in one of the teams you would have a special team sweater which was really quite the thing. We also had a Sunday uniform. Originally, this was navy blue pleated skirts done onto liberty bodices. I can't think what we used to have on top because you couldn't tuck a shirt in, could you? When I was about twelve, we had new uniforms. They chose a sort of maroon wool dress with a dropped waist and pleats. You had all these great pleats around your hips and it was the most unflattering, hot, sweaty and ghastly coloured dress you could possibly imagine.

As this was a Catholic boarding school, we went to Mass every day except Saturday and Wednesday when we were allowed to have a lie-in. The nuns liked us to get up and go even these days, but we didn't. We had to wear veils for Mass which we had to make ourselves out of ballet-skirt netting. We would queue up in two's to go to the chapel, which was in the nuns' part of the building. After Mass, there was breakfast. Breakfast was always different on a Sunday because the maids went to church, you see, so we didn't get porridge (Thank God!), we got cornflakes. There was nobody to cook the porridge so I don't know whether these cornflakes were supposed to be a Sunday treat or not. Our maids worked in the kitchen, cooking the food, and in the laundry. They didn't wear any uniform and we didn't really see very much of them. Certainly, they didn't clean the school. *We* cleaned the school. Friday evening was cleaning and mending night. We had to clean our classrooms and took it in turns. We had a mop to mop the lino. It was just a dry mop and, really, we'd just flick it around. We had to dust as well. It was quite nice cleaning the classrooms because you just went off and flicked the duster around, and then we'd all play. Since the school was an enormous building with several staircases, we could play hide-and-seek or run. It was good fun. Nobody seemed to be supervising us doing our cleaning. We always had to do our mending too, darning our socks. It was good training, I suppose, but who darns socks today? I don't, I just chuck them away.

The nuns had a joined-on but separate building where they lived. We used to see some of their items of clothing hanging out to dry and there were some peculiar ones. We did wonder what they were for. They had flat pieces of white linen with little tapes and I think they put them on to flatten their bosoms because they all had very flat fronts, even the busty ones. Perhaps they felt it was going a bit too far to wear bras but it was probably more comfortable to wear that than nothing at all. Or perhaps it was for humiliation. When I first arrived, the nuns wore coifs which had very hard pieces of stiffened material biting into their foreheads and the great long coif hanging down. They later changed to veils, but even then they had the stiff bit and you could see sometimes it was so tight their heads were very sore. Some of the nuns slept in the dormitory as we couldn't be left alone all night.

The day started at six forty-five a.m. and one of the nuns didn't ring a bell or anything, she stood by your bed (she must have enjoyed this) and she would say. 'Good morning, Flora' in a very cheery, musical voice. Of course, I couldn't hear it at first and then gradually I'd focus. There she'd be, smiling away: 'Good morning, Flora.' Certainly, when we were in the big dormitory there used to be a bell rung all up and down to wake everybody. We had to leap up smartly. There was a lavebo with a red stone floor and basins down each side. At the far end there were four cubicles which didn't have curtains. They were only for washing your feet. And down the middle there was a locker where you kept all your things.

We used to have hairwashing night on Saturdays. Some girls did have long hair but it had to be plaited. I wore my hair straight and short and the boarding mistress used to cut it. We used to queue up to have our hair dried because no one in those days had a personal hair-dryer. There was this one great big hair-dryer and I sat in the chair and the nun dried my hair, sort of, and off I went and the next one sat down. Every now and again, a nun would go through your hair with a nit comb but I never remember having to wash with special shampoo or anything. Perhaps we did and didn't know it. Originally there were four baths in cubicles and they would be going all the time. There would be a rota and you had two baths a week. It probably wasn't physically possible to fit us girls through any more. And of course, as we got older we wanted more baths. In order to fit us all in, we only had a quarter of an hour for a bath each and what we used to do is split it between two girls. We didn't realize we were using up all the hot water and I suppose that by the time the older ones got in, the water had gone cold.

The only man in the school was the gardener and he was quite old. Obviously, the priests used to come for Mass and to give us talks. May was the procession season. We used to go down to the Catholic church in our veils, and we set off – along with the Legion of Mary and the Mothers of This, the Young Men of That – and would process up from the church, led by the priest and the altar boys with candles and swinging incense, all singing hymns all up the roads of Bedford! In the beginning, it was quite fun. Then it got to be a bit of a bore and eventually I was slightly embarrassed. We seemed to accept the religion because it was there. The majority of girls at the school were not actually Catholic. The thing was that the non-Catholic boarders had to go to Mass on Sunday and that was understood, but they didn't go during the week. We had Benediction on Sunday and everyone went to that because it was a social occasion. I think the non-Catholics also went on the processions, although they must have thought them peculiar.

We didn't have many outings at school. There was the furniture museum in Bedford where we sometimes went to draw furniture. We also had great trips to the cemetery which was a favourite – to go around the cemetery and read all the gravestones of all the little children who had died and see who had flowers. I loved going round the graveyard. Every Saturday and Sunday, we went for walks for miles and miles in a crocodile. I quite enjoyed that. We wore panama hats in the summer and velour hats in the winter. They were quite flattering, those hats, and we liked them. And when you got in the netball team, you went off to play against other teams.

We played hockey, netball and tennis at school. We'd play netball as often as we could because you could play that in the school. Hockey never really got off the ground because the playing-fields were over a mile from the school and we would have to walk to get there. The fields were often flooded in winter. They were all right in the summer for the tennis but they weren't really much good for hockey. I remember once just as someone was about to hit the ball, I slipped in the mud and got hit with it right on the temple. It was wonderful. I came out all purple and was quite the celebrity for days. The nuns didn't call a doctor, just put some witch-hazel on it and took me home. Once in netball, I fell over and knocked myself out. I couldn't have been out more than a second or so but they took me to hospital and I really liked going. I felt fine and it was just so exciting. Also, I used to have chilblains. Sometimes they were so bad I had to wear slippers to school and in the end, I was taken to the doctor and had to have tablets. I noticed that a certain time after I took them, about an hour, they would start speeding up the circulation and I'd go all mottled and purple and stingy and prickly, like prickly heat. I used to take them an hour before the Latin lesson and then say I didn't feel well. The nun would say, 'Oh, dear child, go and lie down!' And I'd get off!

These illnesses and injuries were great occasions. The school had a special sick room. When I used to get tonsillitis, I would just stay in the dorm but if you had glandular fever, or if they didn't know what was wrong with you, you were isolated. Anything that was different from the usual was nice. And you would get special food. Often it was my birthday when I was ill with tonsillitis and they would send up marshmallows. When it was your birthday, your parents would send food or money and you would choose your friends for a party at a separate table in the dining room.

Dad was a Wing Commander when I was quite small and we lived in Yorkshire, then Lincolnshire, then all sorts of places. I found it very exciting. I used to love it but I'm sure my mother hated all the moving around. It was wonderful going somewhere different and seeing a new house. Of course, sometimes the houses were exactly the same, but they were still different because they were in a completely new place with an unexplored garden. I'm the eldest of five. My sister is the next one down – she's four years younger – and I have three brothers: Christian, then Angus, and James, who is thirteen years younger than me. I don't know what they thought when he came along, but I had a very happy childhood. It was all lovely.

I used to boss the others around. In some ways I liked being the eldest because I could say, 'I'm the head teacher and you all have to do this', and I used to arrange them and make them do things I wanted. But on the other hand, it was difficult because I used to have to help wash up when they were considered too young and I would have to fight all the battles about wearing high heels. It follows much more easily for the second one. I used to fight with my sister physically. She was stronger than I was, though she was younger and smaller. They were horrible to me, those children! They used to say, 'Oh, Flora's and Ella's names should be turned around because then it could be Elephant Ella and Fairy Flora!'; because, you see, I was so much bigger. And then we would all get in the car, or rather *they* would get in the car and when I was going to get in, they'd say, 'Oh, careful, careful!' and all these horrid things. Our cars were something. At one point we had a Rolls Royce but usually everybody else's car was smarter than ours. We had a Wolsey and the petrol tank fell off it in Princes Risborough High Street. The door fell off once. The Rolls Royce was a most beautiful old car, a sporting model, and it overhung the pavement by about six foot. There wasn't room for the whole family in it because its cab was very small. I suppose like all men, my father thought just once in his life he would have a wonderful car. He ran over our silver teapot with it! I can't think how he afforded it. You aren't rich in the Forces, not with five children at boarding school.

Dad was pleasant but not a push-over. He wasn't authoritarian or domineering. On Sunday mornings, he used to try and organize us to do jobs. There was a phase of that. When he'd want somebody, he'd say, 'Christian, Angus, James, err, Flora, Ella' because he used to get our names muddled, there were so many. As a family we were always very unpunctual and it used to drive him mad because of his military background. My mother is the most unpunctual person and we must have taken after her.

There was always a batman or batwoman to help in the house and when we were young, Mother also had a live-in girl. I'm not surprised really. When I was older, in desperation sometimes, Mother and I used to lure all the little ones out into the garden and rush back in and shut all the doors so we could have a bit of peace and quiet. We never had a television and I used to annoy the neighbours by going round and asking if I could watch theirs. What I didn't realize until later on was that they used to hate me coming round because I would get so excited, I'd say, 'Oh, look at this!' and 'Oh, see what's going to happen now!', and ruin their viewing. I have no idea why we didn't have a television except a lot of people didn't.

Only once do I remember rationing. I had what would now be called a rather streetwise friend. We must have been very small and she had this idea about swapping Coke bottles for coupons. I know my husband used to swap all his sweet ration or his coupons, whatever they had at his school, for marbles. He would not eat sweets so he could swap them for everything else. I don't remember having any coupons at all but then I never went shopping with my mother when I was little.

Our houses were all fairly large. The pre-war big old gracious houses were lovely but the modern ones were not as interesting. I think they were doled out according to rank, the CO getting the biggest, nicest house on the station. One family had so many children that they had to have two houses, a pair of semis. It was a nice life on the stations because when you got a bicycle, you could ride around quite safely, there was no worry about anything or anyone. There were Christmas parties for us children and dances when we got older. Because everybody knew each other, you always had friends. We'd be three or four years at each station and would have people to stay in the holidays from school. There were always tennis courts and nice things you could do. We all played a lot of tennis and I was in the tennis team. I don't have a lot of stamina and if it was very very hot, I used to flake out before the end of the match. The uniform white tennis dress was as short as anything we used to wear in the Sixties, and in the holidays I would go and play in tournaments and even mixed doubles with a carroty-haired bloke and used to always wear that type of dress. We had proper Dunlop tennis shoes and a heavy gut-strung wooden-framed racquet.

At home during the holiday we all used to sit round and listen to the radio. There were all these silly programmes like *Ray's a Laugh*, which was on at Sunday lunch-times, and *The Navy Lark*. I used to listen to *Children's Hour* and *Larry the Lamb*. We used to love it. There was a play called *Mossy Green Theatre* and it was introduced by some lovely lovely music which I found out later was *The Jewels of the Madonna*. I used to listen out for that. My parents would sit and listen with us and when I first married it was a habit I kept on. We didn't have a television at first and listened to plays and *The Archers*. Jeremy and I finally broke the Archers habit, deciding we would never listen to them again. We haven't!

Christmas was pretty chaotic really. Father Christmas went on coming for a long time, James being thirteen years younger than me. First of all, we used to put Dad's rugger socks at the end of the bed and used to get a tangerine in the bottom, but as the boys came along this turned into a pillowcase and we seemed to get rather more. When it got to the stage of me being rather more grown-up than the others, I used to help my parents sort them out. My mother was terrible about Christmas presents. Relations used to send packages and she would put them in her cupboard. Well, I was an ace at opening things and getting them back without being discovered but the trick was I knew what was in them. I suppose I was about fourteen when one pair of stockings appeared from Aunt Betty, I *knew* there had been two but it was a question of whether I was going to give myself away. I suppose my mother got desperate one day, and as she had obviously looked in the presents herself, she just helped herself to mine!

We had the traditional Christmas lunch but later on we used to have Christmas dinner and all get dressed up in evening gear. We used to go to church. I remember one Christmas we actually went to my father's church because he wasn't Catholic and this was rather nice. He was Anglican and went to the one on the station. In fact, there was always a C of E church on the station and I think always a Catholic one as well. Mother did all the Christmas cooking herself. The trouble was we were quite undisciplined and used to help ourselves to bits, which must have driven her mad. Later on when I was looking after the others and was pregnant, I would stagger home from the city with this and that to cook something up and find that they had eaten all the recipe ingredients when they had got up at about midday. I suppose it must have driven Mum crackers. It's just as well she wasn't strict. And when Father was a bit more elevated, we were supplied with a cook. This was terrible because he wanted to cook us big lunches of Brown Windsor soup and roast chicken and all we wanted was boiled eggs. To make sure he had everything on time, he would put the electric stove on at about eleven o'clock. In fact, in the end, he went back to the Mess because it was ridiculous. It just didn't work out, our family was too chaotic. My father did very well and ended up as Air Vice-Marshall.

Only once did we go on holiday and that was a day trip to St Leonard's-on-Sea! That was the only holiday away I remember. I suppose the idea of taking five children somewhere was daunting. Can you imagine? I don't think I would have bothered. We were all perfectly happy roaming around the station and really, coming from boarding school, it was a holiday just to be home so we didn't actually ever go anywhere else, even to stay with relatives. My father's relatives were all in South Africa, anyway, so there was no question of going to see them. I had an aunt in Scotland but we didn't go and plonk ourselves on her. She had polio and wasn't very fit. My mother had a funny family. Her eldest sister had two boys. They came to stay with us once and we used to sew up their pyjamas and give them apple-pie beds. They never came again! I don't think she got on badly with her relatives but they were never in much contact. She had an elder brother, Uncle Nigel, who used to come and visit us at school sometimes and take us out for Sunday with 'Auntie' this or 'Auntie' that – always a different 'Auntie' – which was very nice. We never saw anything of him otherwise. The younger one, Aunt Shirley, who was an actress and rather eccentric, was the one we saw most of but she married a Czech and they moved to Strasbourg so that was that. We used to act things out as a family. There was a famous acting out of 'Aunt Shirley saying goodbye at Doncaster Station' and we took it in turns to be Aunt Shirley because she was greatly theatrical. Once, she had us all lined up on the platform and said, 'Goodbye, Flora, kiss kiss kiss' and then, 'Goodbye, Ella, kiss kiss kiss' and then, suddenly, a whistle blew and she threw her hands up screaming and rushed up the platform thinking she was missing her train and it wasn't hers at all! We still sometimes enact it.

And when James was a baby we used to put him on a whoopee cushion! It really used to amuse us. My mother even did it too, we thought this was hysterical. My mother also went through an outrageous phase when we were living in France. She used to get the English papers and there used to be these weird advertisements for liquefied seaweed and elevator shoes. She used to send them off to people! My father used to get so annoyed. He'd yell, 'This is costing me a fortune!' But we used to just howl. When I got back to school I started doing it too.

At half-term I used to go and stay with friends. One half-term we used to go Pete Moon hunting, which meant we would look for this certain boy who went to one of the boys' schools in Bedford. Susan, the friend I stayed with, lived in Bletchley and Pete Moon used to go on the same train as her as he lived in the same village. We all fancied him – he looked a bit like Adam Faith. I used to borrow her brother's bicycle and we would go on this Pete Moon hunt and catch a glimpse of him if we were lucky. We did speak to him occasionally and sent him something odd out of the ads in the papers as well!

We thought boys were Very Desirable Objects from about thirteen or fourteen. I was quite shy and never had a lot of luck with these boys. We did have a combined school dance with a boys' school, once, which was amazing, going all the way to Radcliffe to this Catholic school run by monks. We went there first and then they came back to us. In the early days when there was a lot of Joe Loss dance music around, and as we didn't have a lot to do in the evening, the older girls would teach the younger ones how to dance. Real ballroom dancing. And it is very rare, really, to find a man who can dance nicely which is such a shame because all of us could dance so well. My husband can't do it. I remember when the Shake came out, Jeremy couldn't even shake! We had the record-player on Saturday evenings and even Sundays – they weren't strict in saying we couldn't dance on Sunday. When our homework was done we all went and danced around the hall. I really liked it. We used to take turns being the man.

We never went out to the cinema but used to have films in the hall. This would have been on weekends and they would screen *David Copperfield* or *Great Expectations* or *Oliver Twist* – all the Dickens – and Jane Austen's *Pride and Prejudice.* For some reason we were allowed to go and see *Spartacus* and I can't imagine why they thought that would be so good but we liked it. It must have been because it was to do with the Christians. We also had *The Robe*. Robert Taylor, sigh.

I can't remember how old I was when I confronted the then boarding mistress with why we weren't allowed to use Tampax. Apparently the Church was against it. She wasn't very good at explaining things. She probably didn't know herself. This nun was the chemistry teacher and a real innocent. I remember reading *Love in a Cold Climate* once and she came round and said, 'Oh, I don't think you should be reading *that*!' I said that it was only Nancy Mitford. She clearly had no idea who Nancy Mitford was and was just reacting to the 'Love' in the title. Then she said, 'Well, read it quickly and put it away.' In fact, my sister upset them by reading *Go Tell It On The Mountain* and *The Fire Next Time* by James Baldwin. I think she got thrown out! There was The List of banned books, you see, though I'm sure Nancy Mitford wasn't on it.

My mother did have a rather embarrassing talk with me at one stage about menstruation but we never talked about anything else. We had a film at school in biology which was like a text book with drawings but it certainly didn't show people. That put at rest your ideas of how a baby actually got out but I am not sure we covered really how it got in. We girls used to talk about it at night. I used to worry about all sorts of peculiar things, like bodily hair, and whether it was all right, because you never saw anybody else naked to know. Periods were such a nuisance, such a palaver because of those ghastly things around your waist which were so uncomfortable and always got twisted up. I couldn't imagine what it was like to be a Victorian woman and how they ever did anything. Reading about so-called primitive tribes, where women were put in huts because they were thought unclean or whatever, I think must have been the best possible thing – a nice quiet dark place, let off your duties until you felt well again. They aren't daft. We bought our sanitary towels at the chemist and they used to come in these blue packets with rather nice blue paper but I am sure the nuns must have bought them for the younger ones who had started. You would have had to ask for them. Your peer group would talk about the facts of life. The older girls didn't tell you anything, and really, I suppose, that is how you got the knowledge, from girls who were a bit more advanced than you. There were two loos outside the big dormitory and only one had an incinerator so here was a big problem! When you started, you were very conscious of it and found it all rather embarrassing. If there was a queue for the loo, you used to think that everyone will know when you won't use *that* one. We actually really minded. It was so odd when you consider we were all girls.

We never thought about the nuns as private people. They were nuns and had always been there. We took them for granted. I do remember going on about my height once because I have been the same height since I was about twelve. I used to be the tallest at five foot, three inches, and by the time I was fourteen I was the shortest. I complained to the then boarding mistress, 'Can you imagine, I'm only five foot three!' And she said, 'I'm only five foot two, you know.' So I said, 'Well, yes, but you're a nun, you can offer it up!' I went through a phase at thirteen when I was terribly terribly rude to them. Other girls must have been awful, too, because you do get like that at adolescence. What used to happen is if you did something naughty, you would get a black mark and on Friday evening after supper the Reverend Mother would come in and she would read out the list of people who had black marks. When she called your name you had to stand up and she would say, 'What have you got a black mark for?' That in itself, having to stand up in front of everybody and say what you had done, was awful. The other girls didn't censure you, though, for a black mark. It was thought quite bold.

We used to have quite a lot of midnight feasts. In the early days when we were young and didn't have much access to money, it might only be a bottle of tonic water and a box of Maltesers. Once we went off to the science lab to consume that. It was just the fun of going somewhere. When we were older, I do remember that we laid on this real spread. There was one girl whose parents made parsnip wine so we had some and we had real goodies like chocolates and chickens and cakes. We all crept down to the cellar and just as we got there, down came the nun who used to wake us up by saying, 'Good morning, whatever-your-name-is!' I suppose she was a light sleeper and had heard us. The punishment was that all our food was given to the juniors. The next day we all had to have school supper and those juniors sat there and ate our food! Oh, that was mean!

There was always a 'phase' going on with school meals. Behind the pavilion, there was a patch of land where the school grew vegetables. You always knew what was growing because you had it all the time. You might start off with clove and rhubarb jam and as the season waned it ended up being just clove jam which wasn't very exciting. You could also tell what they bought in job lots because we might get, say, boiled chestnuts quite a lot. Winkles we had, ugh, for quite a few days running.

I said we always had porridge for breakfast, and toast. Sometimes we had fried bread but not very often. It was quite full of fat and we used to have it with marmalade on top. Can you imagine it? Quite extraordinary. But then all the food was stodgy. The meat was the usual done-to-death beef or it might have been lamb. It was hard to tell what it was. We could tell when it was chicken, though. And cabbage and parsnips, or swedes. I know they were very cheap but I literally cannot swallow parsnips, they make me quite sick. I hated the swedes too but at least I could eat them. There was a lot of passing plates under the table if you could find anyone who liked what you didn't. We had to eat everything and were made to stay until we did. If it was lunch and it was time to go into class and you still hadn't finished they took it away. They would never produce it the next day or the next meal. Your playtime had gone and I suppose that was considered enough.

There was no food that the school did well expect for the sweets – chocolate splodge and squashed fly biscuits and sago.

I was a very poor eater. The head girl and I were always the last in the dining room. We couldn't eat it. I remember my mother never gave us cabbage at home because I couldn't stand it but once she forgot and I could not reconcile it with the stuff we had at school. It wasn't gritty and dark and bitter and horrible. It was the same with lettuce. I always used to wonder where the middle of the lettuce went. I can't think that the nuns ate it because surely they were mortifying the flesh!

We used to get the post with breakfast. The best day was Valentine's day, February the fourteenth, and one year the nun came in and she gave out all the letters and nobody, but nobody, had a Valentine card. Well, what a load of glum faces. Then she went off and came back in with a stack so high! I got a real Valentine only once, not one sent as a joke. Some girls got loads. I remember getting a letter from a boy at school once. I thought this was wonderful. He said in it, 'The weather is bloody.' Well, for me this was really a good letter. I think he was at Sandhurst at the time. The thought of boys was quite nice and when we went out on Saturday mornings to the Baked Spud for a cup of coffee, we'd view a few. There were one or two I knew and if I caught a glimpse of them that would keep me going for a week.

I suppose we all expected to get married except for the few who decided to become nuns. The tearaway of the school became a nun. She was a couple of years older than me and her mother had died when she was quite young. She was really very naughty but I am not quite sure what she used to do as it was usually shrouded in mystery – we weren't meant to follow her example. She used to escape down the fire-escape and go off. But, quite amazingly, she became a nun. We always said we would have a school reunion but we never did and I do regret it because the school doesn't exist any more. It is still a school, now a big comprehensive, but the nuns sold up. These nuns were

Daughters of the Holy Ghost, which was a French order that had come over to England, and there were still a few French nuns who were incredibly strict compared to the nice English nuns. If you didn't go to Mass, you had a period for doing your homework in the mornings and it was often desperately necessary to do this. It wasn't so much frowned on when you skived off but that you felt you shouldn't somehow miss Mass. They weren't always on about God by any manner of means. There was one girl, a non-Catholic, who at about the age of eleven was incredibly keen to convert and they actually advised her parents to take her away. The nuns felt she was an emotional girl and was far too young for them to be influencing her. So she had to go to a different sort of school. We went to confession to confess being nasty to someone or telling lies, or not doing our homework. The priest must have got terribly bored listening to us girls.

I actively thought that I wouldn't have sex until I got married and most of the other girls thought that too. When I got to Paris, I kept in contact with a girl who informed me that her father (her mother was dead) had worried about her first sexual encounter so he had arranged for his best friend to go to bed with her. Can you imagine? This would have been the early Sixties at that point. The reason given was that it would be pleasant and she wouldn't be frightened. I thought this most peculiar and outrageous but most people even today would. I believe totally in the power of love and am still very sentimental. I cry at sad books and plays.

The nuns were quite narrow in some ways. I do remember once practising the piano and there were always net curtains halfway up the windows. There was some exciting noise going on outside so I got up on the piano stool to have a peer and one of the nuns came in and said, 'Get down from that piano stool. It is not ladylike to stand on a piano stool and look out the window!' We were not allowed to run in the corridors and our table manners were supervised (I wish they were at my daughters' school) and we would never go out without our hats and gloves on or without having clean shoes. We had to be neat and tidy and got bad marks if we didn't have our ties on or something was crooked. When we went for a walk in a crocodile or were going to the playing-fields, we had to walk properly and not leap about. Everything had to be done in a ladylike manner. I am surprised they didn't march us. To be fair, though, when we got to large open spaces on the hills, then we were allowed to roam around. Again, we were not allowed to eat in the street. Even to this day, I find even if I am very hungry and rushing around somewhere I don't feel right if I munch my sandwich in public. I remember saying 'bloody' in school a few times and got told off for it. 'Bloody hell' was the bad thing we used to say, which is not nearly as bad as my daughters say today. I certainly swear more as I've got older but it is more acceptable now, anyway. At school we used to do some quite good plays and if someone had to say a bad word in a speech we'd all be waiting for it.

By the late Fifties, we put curlers in our hair every night. They were big metal ones with plastic wire or ones with spikes sticking out which you would roll up and stick a hair clip in. You had to roll them tight because they would slip out. It may seem funny that we would go to all this trouble and agony when it was just girls but I suppose we took pride in our appearance, although we weren't allowed to wear make-up at school. I remember one day I was going out and had forgotten to curl my hair, so I put the curlers in that morning and asked the boarding mistress if it would be all right if I wore them for breakfast. Would you believe it, she said 'Yes'! But the senior girls were outraged at this. They were not pleased. Wearing curlers in the dining room!

We used to play cards in the common room, rummy for instance, and the younger ones used to do stencils or painting by numbers, which you would get for your birthday. The sixth-formers had a new classroom all to themselves and they were allowed to paint murals on the wall. These were so good the girls were then allowed to paint murals on the dining room, which I felt was rather go-ahead. One of the girls painted a picture you used to see on biscuit boxes of two horses, a white one and another one standing the opposite way and it was rather windy as though they were on the edge of a cliff. It was absolutely beautiful.

I never remember being homesick at school, I thoroughly enjoyed it. But by the time I was sixteen I had had enough. Although we were allowed out in the mornings down the town and although there was a common room, you couldn't even have a cup of tea when you wanted one. I found that very irksome at the time, so, wanting to do languages, I decided to leave. From the minute I had my first French lesson I knew that was what I liked and I don't know what I would have done if my parents had not been in France at the time I left school. I would have done something with languages in any event but I probably would have done something rather more formal than live in France with my parents and study at the Sorbonne. At first, I thought I would like to be an interpreter but I couldn't have done the seven years of study. Men are conditioned to do that because they have to go on the rest of their lives working. They have a terrible burden of responsibility in many ways I think. They aren't free. And having a family can be a terrific drain on a man even if he is desperately fond of them. I have often thought a house and school fees are a terrible burden to a man, and to think that he might feel like chucking it up tomorrow but can't do it. If you stop earning, it's a disaster. There are compensations for me not having a career. Since the girls are older and at school, I have had a wonderful life so I don't complain. I used to of course!

There was only one girl in school who I really didn't like. Unfortunately, she was in my form. The thing was that in school a year makes a real difference so usually you hung out with your own form. Of course, we all used to get together for the dancing and when I first went the young ones would have 'Angels' who were older girls to look after them and do their mending. Luckily, by the time I got old enough this was no longer going on. I don't know who took care of 'the babies'. Of course, girls had crushes on other girls and we used to get a lecture every now and then about how silly it was. I had crushes on two girls and it was just a substitute because there were no boys about. It was the same thing as Pete Moon hunting – getting a glimpse and getting rather silly – and I am sure it was extremely irritating for the girls to be so followed around. The best thing was to ignore it and for the most part the nuns did. Eventually the crush would fade away and you'd think, Blimey, what on earth was all that about? It just added a bit of spice to a quite boring and safe life.

My parents were always Conservatives but I wasn't interested in politics growing up. We were vaguely aware of what was going on in the world but I am sure I didn't really understand any issues. We didn't have television or newspapers at school, although some girls had their own radios which were used exclusively for listening to pop music. I think I only knew about Suez and other issues from later on, in retrospect. I knew the Coronation was going on, though, because we had a special day at school. They got a telly in and we watched the pomp and then had a celebration meal. One of the teachers said to me, 'You should have told us your second name was Elizabeth, we could have called you Elizabeth after our dear Queen!' I didn't think much of that! I rather fancied my own name at the time.

Learning history at school, we seemed to concentrate on the Catholic view, the dissolution of the monasteries and Henry the Eighth. I remember later on realizing how extremely ignorant I was, even about Disraeli and certainly anything more recent than Disraeli. I had no idea even how the First World War started. In fact, I still feel I have a big gap in general world history. I do have ideas and opinions, now, but didn't then. Everything was done by grown-ups and didn't really apply to me. But things are different today. When I took Caroline into school last year, they were talking about not allowing Yasir Arafat into the United Nations and she thought that was scandalous. She said, 'What is the point of the UN if someone can't go in and speak there?' So girls are much more politically aware today. I remember when Caroline was at baby school, they were taught about Pol Pot and I wasn't sure that for three-year-olds it was quite the thing! The one issue we were really concerned about at school was The Bomb and we had great discussions about it. I don't know how we knew so much about it all but we did, even though we weren't reading newspapers at school.

Looking back, I'm sure this was laying the foundations for a big excuse for doing whatever we felt like because we were threatened by The Bomb. It was a bit like the war feeling, giving you an excuse to do things that perhaps you otherwise wouldn't have had the courage to do. We were worried about it, though. Caroline, my thirteen-year-old, wants to ban The Bomb. We thought, as girls, it was all getting a bit dangerous but didn't want to ban it, not just yet, anyway. Intellectually, we weren't up to any real argument and hadn't the experience to reason it out. It was also our conservative backgrounds. My father was very good at explaining his point of view.

I don't know what I thought of beatniks. Of course, I never was one. In a way, I sort of admired them, and certainly didn't dislike them, but we wanted to get on and 'do something' and that lifestyle seemed rather negative. You didn't condemn people for having those thoughts or feelings, but it never was for me.

I was very embarrassed the first time I went to the cinema with a boy. I was about thirteen. Well, I was *with* this boy, but actually we went with his sister and her boyfriend and some others, so it wasn't such a date. The only coat I had to wear was my school coat, my great big navy blue school coat, and school socks. And his sister was rather glamorous being seventeen-and-a-half. But I never said to my mother that I needed a coat and I don't think I ever realized, until the situation arose, what clumsy great things those coats were. Towards the end of the Fifties I was certainly aware of fashion, the bouffant hairdos with all that backcombing. We used to do it and it looked like nothing on earth. You had bits hanging down at the side and then would backcomb a bit and throw it up like a coxcomb, but I didn't use hairspray.

We used to get clothes in Marks & Spencer or some other chain store. I started making clothes myself when I was about ten and would buy things in little shops when I was allowed out later on. By the time I was fourteen, it got more difficult because there were all these stiff petticoats which you really couldn't make yourself. My first grown-up dress was one I wore to a dance on the station for the teenagers. That was turquoise, gathered at the waist. It was sleeveless with a tight-fitting bodice and a high boat neckline. My first high heels were white and I did want them. They weren't really high, just seemed it, and my mother bought them for me. I wouldn't wear white shoes now because my feet are rather big. My second pair were slightly higher and were suede. They could only be worn during the holidays. The big deal at school was when you were allowed to wear slip-ons on Sundays, rather than lace-ups or sandals. That was at thirteen. We wore beige knee-length socks for school and, strangely, two pairs of knickers – navy bags, and what we called 'linings', which were white ones. I don't know why. We changed our underwear only twice a week! The laundry came back in big baskets. Later on, we only had to wear two pairs for games and I suppose that was because our divided skirts were rather short. At home, my mother didn't have a washing-machine until my brother Angus was born and did quite a lot of washing in the bath. There were no laundrettes. She didn't boil anything except the nappies. Much of the big stuff, like sheets, would have gone out to a laundry but the bath was always full of underclothes.

We liked the stiff petticoats. Sometimes they were net ones and sometimes they were hooped. They weren't comfortable but comfort wasn't something you took into consideration. I remember being taken by two of the older girls at school to buy my first stockings, which entailed buying a suspender belt. They took me to the local store and they were divided in their opinions as to how I should spend my money. One of them said I ought to have a

cheap suspender belt with lots of pairs of cheap stockings
and the other said, 'No, it's her first one; she ought to have
an expensive suspender belt and a couple of pairs of really
nice stockings.' Then the first girl said, 'Oh, she'll only
ladder them!' I didn't get the prettiest suspender belt but I
did get some decent stockings which, of course, I did
ladder immediately. They were so uncomfortable. It was
such a relief when the Sixties came and you could put
tights on. The tops of the stockings were always cutting in
but we didn't care. We'd do anything to look 'the thing'.
When the new tennis dresses came in, they were ones
without sleeves. There was a girl who was older than me
and she had these great tufts of ginger hair sticking out
from under her arms and I thought, I am not going to be
like that!, so I made enquiries and managed to get myself
a ladies' razor for my legs and under my arms. One of the
fashionable girls at school had eyelash curlers and she
would lend them so we could curl our eyelashes, which was
more bending, really. The nuns wouldn't let us do
anything outrageous but they weren't actually aware of
the extent of our experimenting.

When we had the dances at the station, they'd have
both records and a live band. We weren't very hot on
alcohol. The first thing I drank was beer. It was a question
of expense. The boys I went around with weren't very rich
and they all drank beer so everybody drank beer and I got
to quite like it. I felt rock 'n' roll and skiffle was wonderful.
We listened to Lonnie Donnegan. He wasn't a great pin-
up, of course, but the music was quite nice. And Paul
Anka and Adam Faith. Certainly, Craig Douglas and Cliff
Richard were very popular. We didn't see these pop stars
as people we would ever meet and never even expected to
catch a glimpse of such exalted personages. We loved
Richard Burton, Robert Taylor and Deborah Kerr. Colin
MacInnes's *Absolute Beginners* is just about right – all
these ghastly teenagers screeching and making a noise. It
must have been, I suppose, because teens had some
money. You only get pandered to by the media and shops
if you have money to spend. I used to spend my money on

pop star magazines and would sometimes buy a bottle of salad cream to put on the horrible salad! But really, at school it was a question of only a little pocket money.

I did envy the friends of mine on the camp who got themselves jobs at Christmas taking letters round and who were quite lively. It was lack of confidence on my part. Being in a convent school like that, I was very confident within my group but hadn't any experience with real people. I thought the children on the camps, who didn't go to boarding school, were rather more with it and had more parties. I was invited to everything when I was home as people were very nice, but I felt quite left out because I didn't know anyone well. I remember one party in particular when I was about sixteen. It was on New Year's Eve and there were lots of people there. I knew quite a number of them by sight but I didn't really know them. The elder brother of the bloke who was giving the party went out at midnight and came in first-footing, saying he was going to kiss all the girls. I was acutely embarrassed. I really did not want him to kiss me because I had never kissed anybody, and especially in front of all these people I didn't know. I was dreading it. He got nearer and nearer and I suppose I must have been so nervous that the very worst possible thing happened. He gave me a kiss and said, 'Oh, dear, that wasn't a good one!' It was terrible. Can you imagine it? It wasn't even a real kiss. I suppose he realized he wasn't going to get a 'real' kiss out of me. I wouldn't have even known then what a real kiss was! It was really frightfully embarrassing. There were three brothers in that house quite near us and this brother would have been about twenty. The others were eighteen and fifteen. I'd have fancied any of them! I often found then, and a bit later, that boys did like me but they were always the younger ones who I didn't like, the really smarty ones I fancied didn't seem to have any interest in me. The traumas of it all! I never had my heart broken, though. It was all just mild flirtation and they all were unobtainable.

One girl at school did have a serious boyfriend. He came to Bedford and we were all frightfully envious. I think he was in the Army and we all talked about it but I am sure the nuns didn't know. We were at the stage when we were allowed out on Saturday mornings and this girl made a rendezvous and off she went. We felt she was incredibly bold. That was something special and we knew he really existed because we caught a glimpse of him. There was also a very glamorous girl who was really large and her mother was very big but also very glamorous. I was quite large at that stage and remember thinking, Goodness, this is a really glamorous girl and she is not as thin as a rake the way they all try and tell you you should be. She used to jet-set off to Switzerland. As far as I am aware, nobody ever made up any boyfriends or said they had wonderful adventures with men although you might expect it in a boarding school. So where were all these boys flashing about on motorbikes and demanding sex. They weren't in my neck of the woods. They were probably older than us at that time.

I am sure my background was privileged. Things were very happy, and right up to this date I often think there must be something dreadful around the corner for me because life has been so pleasant and easy. I can't quite believe there is nothing horrible in store. This is the other side of the coin: you do feel privileged and unfortunately then go around feeling guilty about it, which is a waste of time. We were constantly making things and collecting things at school to send out to poor people. Some of the nuns were missionaries. I don't approve of missionaries although they have the best of motives. They just ruin the people and tell them all their beliefs are wrong and they must believe what you believe – what a cheek! I didn't think about that then because I took everything as it was presented to me. I think I still believe in Hell as I think it is probably only fair! There is one teaching I challenged though – we were told that if a woman was having a child and the doctor couldn't save both of them, he must save the child. I always rebelled against that. I don't know whether it was that I would never be the child but even intellectually I couldn't see it. And also, looking from the

Church's point of view, if the child is newly born and is baptized immediately, they say it is going to go straight to Heaven and have a lovely time, so why deprive it? And there is the poor old mum who has no time to do anything on her deathbed and you are depriving the whole family, wrecking all their lives. I haven't kept to my Catholicism really. I do still go to church sometimes but went through a stage of thinking, Well, there is God and there is me and if I want to talk to Him I can talk to Him. In actual fact, I have come to the conclusion that really it is not a bad thing to all get together and give up an hour on a Sunday if you believe in it. I never thought of ending up a saint and certainly never a nun. I used to be worried that I would have a vocation. I remember asking one of the nuns how she knew she was going to be a nun. She said she had this vocation and had this feeling she sort of knew this was what was meant to be. She told me she used to be very naughty and was up on the mat before the Reverend Mother time after time, thinking they would throw her out. They never did and she was sure she had done the right thing. I thought, Oh, Lord, if it is that sort of thing, it can happen to anyone, and I used to be a bit worried that this vocation would sneak up on me and, like her, I would be helpless against this Great Force. I *really* didn't want to be a nun.